N YORK
in your pocket

Travel Publications

MAIN CONTRIBUTORS: Eric and Ruth Bailey

PHOTOGRAPH CREDITS
©Greg Pease/Folio, Inc. front cover. The Travel Library 7,
8, 11, 12, 16, 17, 18, 19, 20,21, 22, 27, 33, 34, 35, 36, 39,
42, 47, 49, 51, 52, 53 (top & bottom), 57, 62, 65, 67, 84,
85, 89, 92, 95, 111, 116, 124; Eye Ubiquitous/B P Adams
83; Eye Ubiquitous/Trevor Clifford 23; Eye Ubiquitous/J
Grau 25, 97, 99; Eye Ubitquitous/Paul Seheult 56 (bot-
tom); Eye Ubiquitous/Selby 104-105; Eye Ubiquitous/ Paul
Thompson back cover, 40, 45, 55, 56 (top), 59; Eye
Ubiquitous/Ian Yates 50, 73, 80, 87; ©Brigitta L.
House/Michelin title page, 5, 9, 24, 31, 60, 86, 90 (top),
91, 103, 109, 113,117,121,126;Bridgeman Art Library 13,
43; Frank Biondo/Picture Perfect 76, 78; Audrey
Gibson/Picture Perfect 63, 68; Allan Montaine/Picture
Perfect 61, 75; NYC & Co. 90 (bottom); NYC Cruise Line
Inc. 29; Allison M. Simpson/Michelin 30.

*Front cover: Empire State Building; back cover: Statue of Liberty;
title page: New York Taxi*

While every effort is made to ensure that the information in this guide is as accurate and up-to-date as
possible, detailed information is constantly changing. The publisher cannot accept responsibility for any
consequences resulting from changes in information, errors or omissions.

MANUFACTURE FRANÇAISE DES PNEUMATIQUES MICHELIN

Place des Carmes-Déchaux – 63000 Clermont-Ferrand (France)

© Michelin et Cie. Propriétaires-Éditeurs 1996

Dépôt légal Avril 96 – ISBN 2-06-650401-7 – ISSN 1272-1689

No part of this publication may be reproduced in any form

without the prior permission of the publisher.

Printed in Spain 1-03/5

MICHELIN TYRE PLC
Travel Publications
The Edward Hyde Building
38 Clarendon Road
WATFORD Herts WD1 1SX - UK
☎ (01923) 415000

MICHELIN TRAVEL PUBLICATIONS
Editorial Department
One Parkway South
GREENVILLE, SC 29615
☎ 1-800 423-0485
TheGreenGuide-us@us.michelin.com

CONTENTS

Introduction 5
How to Use this Guide 6

BACKGROUND
Geography 8
History 12
People and Culture 22

EXPLORING NEW YORK
Must See 26
Introducing New York 28
Manhattan Walks 31
Attractions
  Museums 37
  Churches 44
  Historical/General Interest 46
  Parks and Zoos 60
Beyond Manhattan
  The Bronx 66
  Brooklyn 67
  Queens 69
  Staten Island 70
Family Outings 72
Away From It All 74

ENJOYING YOUR VISIT
Weather 80
Calendar of Events 81
Accommodations 82
Food and Drink 87
Shopping 94
Entertainment and Nightlife 97
Sports 106

A-Z FACTFINDER
The Basics 108
A-Z Information 110

Index 127

STREETS:

Conduit Blvd.	1
Cross County Pkwy.	2
Fort Hamilton Pkwy.	3
Nassau Expwy.	4
New England Thruway	5
Prospect Expwy.	6
Richmond Pkwy.	7
West St.	8
Whitestone Expwy.	9

BRIDGES AND TUNNELS:

Bronx-Whitestone Bridge (Toll)	10
Brooklyn-Battery Tunnel (Toll)	11
Brooklyn Bridge	12
Cross Bay Veterans Memorial Bridge (Toll)	13
George Washington Bridge (Toll)	14
Henry Hudson Bridge (Toll)	15
Holland Tunnel (Toll)	16
Lincoln Tunnel (Toll)	17
Manhattan Bridge	18
Marine Pkwy. Bridge (Toll)	19
Queensboro Bridge	20
Queens-Midtown Tunnel (Toll)	21
Throgs Neck Bridge (Toll)	22
Triborough Bridge (Toll)	23
Verrazano-Narrows Bridge (Toll)	24
Williamsburg Bridge (Toll)	25

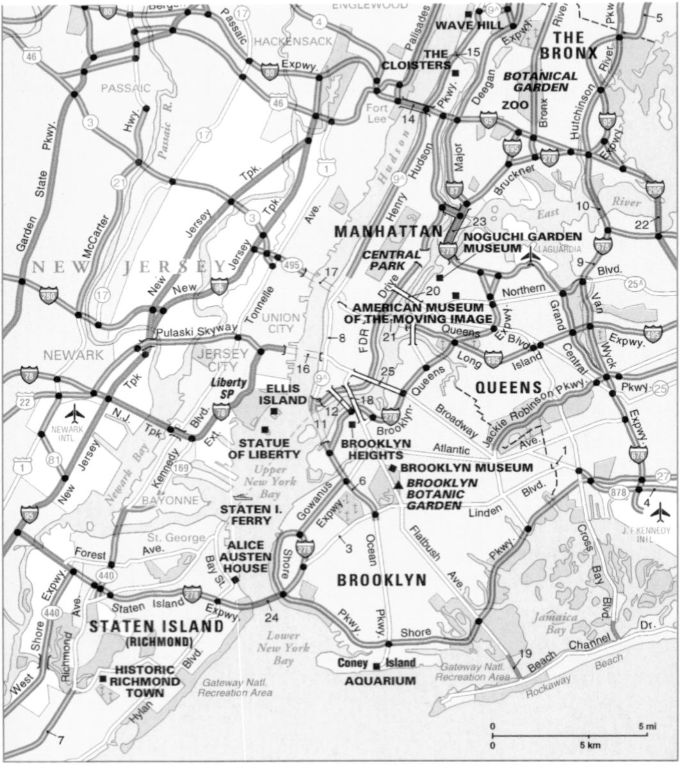

Map showing the five boroughs of New York City.

INTRODUCTION

Anyone visiting New York City for the first time needs boundless energy and the stamina of a long-distance runner. Both large and small screen have provided powerful images of New York that make it seem reassuringly familiar. But only by being there can the visitor experience the unique vitality and legendary pace of "the city that never sleeps." There are a thousand things to do and see, with something to marvel at around every corner. The Statue of Liberty, the street vendors selling their hot dogs and mouthwatering salted pretzels, the canyons of skyscrapers, the swirling crowds of New Yorkers going about their business, all welcome the visitor to the city they refer to with affection and pride as "the Big Apple."

View of Midtown Manhattan from Roosevelt Island.

HOW TO USE THIS GUIDE

This guide is divided into four main sections:

Background sets the scene, with an introduction to New York City's geography and five boroughs, an outline of its rich history from the first settlers, and the people and culture of New York today.

Exploring New York starts by citing the top sights that should be on everyone's checklist. The introduction then describes how the city can be explored. The best way to see Manhattan is on foot, and three suggested walks are given. This is followed by a selection of the main attractions, including the museums and churches. New York is more than the Manhattan skyscrapers, however, so a good selection of other places to visit for every member of the family is included.

Enjoying Your Visit provides friendly, no-nonsense advice on day-to-day activities that can make the difference between a good trip and a great one – eating out, shopping, sports, entertainment and nightlife, as well as information about local events and festivals and the all-important factor, weather.

A-Z Factfinder is an easy-to-use reference section packed with useful information, covering everything you may need to know on your visit, from tipping to renting cars, from using the telephone to vaccinations. A word of warning: opening hours and telephone numbers change frequently, so be sure to check with a local tourist office when planning your visit.

Mounted police patrol New York.

GEOGRAPHY

Situated on the East Coast of the US, New York City borders the Atlantic Ocean. The city occupies the western tip of Long Island, Staten Island, Manhattan Island and a piece of the mainland to the north. The islands, linked by a network of bridges and tunnels, provide protection for one of the largest harbors in the world, ideal for oceangoing vessels.

Manhattan Island, the heart of New York, lies at the head of Upper New York Bay, separated from New Jersey to the west by the Hudson River and from the outer boroughs by the East River and the Harlem River.

The Five Boroughs

Covering a total of 320sq mi, five distinct boroughs combine to form New York City: Manhattan, the Bronx, Brooklyn, Queens

The Hudson River with Manhattan's skyscrapers in the background.

Park Avenue

and Staten Island. (New York City's Greater Metropolitan Area covers 22 counties, including some in adjoining states.)

Manhattan Unarguably the heart of New York, this is where you find all those places made so familiar by film and television. Here are the skyscrapers, theaters, museums and art galleries, as well as Chinatown, Greenwich Village, the East Village, Central Park and Harlem. Manhattan is divided into three major districts. Downtown, the southernmost, extends from the Financial District north to 14th Street. Midtown runs north to the beginning of Central Park at 59th Street. Everything beyond this point forms Uptown or Upper Manhattan.

Above 14th Street, Manhattan is laid out as a grid of avenues and streets. Avenues run north/south and are numbered from First to Twelfth, starting from the east. Streets run east/west, intersecting with the avenues.

There are a few complications, however.
Some avenues have names as well as
numbers; for example, Sixth Avenue is also
called the Avenue of the Americas. Also,
many Downtown streets follow paths that
pre-date the grid plan, and these streets have
names rather than numbers (Bleecker and
Wall streets are two examples).

The Bronx This is the northernmost
borough and the only one on the mainland.
Despite its status as the poorest borough and
its reputation for crime (mainly in the South
Bronx), it contains some of the city's finest
gems, including the Bronx Zoo and the
tranquil New York Botanical Garden.

Brooklyn Located on the western tip of
Long Island, Brooklyn is linked to
Manhattan by three bridges across the East
River, the most famous being the Brooklyn
Bridge. Driving or walking across this
landmark, the visitor will have superb views
of the river and Manhattan. Brooklyn is the
most populous of the five boroughs, with
two and a half million inhabitants. It harbors
many surprises, among them the delightful
Brooklyn Heights Historic District, the 526-
acre Prospect Park and the elegant Brooklyn
Museum on East Parkway.

Queens Adjoining Brooklyn on Long Island,
Queens is most often seen by visitors only on
their way to and from John F. Kennedy
International Airport, which is located in
the borough. Queens was named after
Catherine of Braganza, the wife of Charles II
of England. The US Open Tennis
Championships are held annually in
Flushing Meadows-Corona Park.

*Savor the
excitement of seeing
Manhattan at night
from the 102nd
floor of the
legendary Empire
State Building.*

Staten Island This borough remained largely aloof from the others before 1964, when the Verrazano-Narrows Bridge connected it with Brooklyn. The smallest borough, with about 440,000 inhabitants, it maintains a kind of rural independence and its residents speak of Manhattan as "the city." It can also be reached by the famous Staten Island Ferry, surely one of the world's most spectacular half-hour sightseeing trips and one of the greatest bargains – it's free for pedestrians.

HISTORY

New York's history goes back much further than you might imagine as you stand among its concrete canyons. These sidewalks and skyscrapers are merely the latest chapter in a very long story.

The First People

Long before the arrival of Europeans, the area around the Hudson Valley was occupied by tribes of Indians. The tribes belonged to two major groups, the Algonquian and the Iroquois, who were sworn enemies. Both groups created palisaded, or walled villages. Algonquian tribes first settled the area. They usually lived in wigwams and farmed the land. They kept livestock, grew beans, peas, corn, potatoes, squash and tobacco, and maintained orchards. The Iroquois tribes lived in long, bark-covered houses, giving them the name "People of the Longhouse." They were more aggressive and, although they too farmed, they were primarily hunters. Hostilities between the two native groups continued after the arrival of the Europeans.

New York City skyline.

A detail of a painting in the Metropolitan Museum of Art, by George Bingham, shows fur traders descending the Missouri.

The Early Explorers

The first Europeans to arrive in New York Bay were looking for the Northwest Passage. Giovanni da Verrazano, a Florentine in charge of a French ship, sailed into the bay in 1524. Henry Hudson, an English captain working for the Dutch East India Company, arrived in 1609. Hudson sailed up the river that now bears his name as far as the site of the present-day state capital, Albany. Here, he and his crew traded with the natives who brought skins, fur and fruit.

In 1613 the Dutchman Adriaen Block established a trading post at Fort Nassau, now Albany. Block's ship, *The Tiger*, laden with furs, later caught fire when moored at Manhattan Island. The ship's charred timbers were found when the foundations of the World Trade Center were being dug at Battery Park.

13

The Dutch

The first Dutch settlers sailed for North America in 1614 to establish the colony of New Netherland, which extended from the Delaware to the Connecticut rivers. Eleven years later a permanent settlement was established on Manhattan, which they called New Amsterdam. The colony's director general, Peter Minuit, who left in 1626, bought the island from the Munsee Indians for trinkets worth about $24. At first the Dutch were careful to maintain peace with the Indians for the sake of the furs and other trade goods the tribes brought them. Eventually, acquiring land became the Europeans' main priority – and the Indians occupied much of it. Relations began to deteriorate with the appointment of William Kieft as director general in 1637. He ruthlessly set out to eliminate the natives, first by oppressive taxation and ultimately by encouraging murder. The tribes retaliated and a virtual state of war existed until the mid-1640s.

The Seal of the City of New York.

Peter Stuyvesant, who had had a successful colonial career in Brazil and Curaçao, was appointed director general of the colony in 1647. He was instructed to deal with the Indian "problems" and clean up New Amsterdam, which had acquired a reputation of questionable morality. Under his administration, streets were paved with cobblestones, permanent brick houses were built, gardens were planted and a commercial infrastructure was established. Stuyvesant called for a defensive wall to be built from the Hudson to the East River – the line now followed by Wall Street.

He, too, dealt ruthlessly with the native population. He captured and sold Indians into slavery in the Caribbean, and took Indian children hostage to force their tribes to cooperate with him. He also fomented unrest among the various tribes and used one group to crush another. Although Stuyvesant brought prosperity and stability to the colony, his authoritarian attitudes and religious intolerance to all but the Dutch Reformed Church made him increasingly unpopular.

The British
The British, who were well established along the eastern seaboard, had long coveted New Amsterdam, which they recognized as a potentially important port and as a gateway to the Hudson River and the rich hinterland beyond.

In 1664 they took possession of the city without a fight – its citizens abandoned Stuyvesant's fortifications and welcomed the four invading warships – and renamed it for James, Duke of York, brother of Charles II.

New York flourished under the British, and by 1700 its population had reached 20,000 – a mix of English, Dutch, Irish, French, Germans and Swedes. There was also a growing number of Africans, mostly brought in as slaves.

The American Revolution
Colonists contributed greatly to the British economy, but began to feel isolated. They

A statue of George Washington stands outside the Federal Hall National Memorial where he was sworn in as the first president of the United States.

had no political representation, yet taxes were increasingly imposed upon them. Thousands of British troops were based in the colonies – to be financed by the colonists. Restrictive laws were passed, some limiting trading rights, others forbidding colonists from settling beyond certain areas. In 1775 unrest turned into revolution with the battles of Lexington and Concord in Massachusetts. On July 4, 1776, the Declaration of Independence was adopted.

New York occupied a key position between New England and the southern colonies. During the war, the city served as a major base for the British army and navy. Life in New York became grim. Starvation and disease spread among the population, now swollen to 30,000 by troops, prisoners and refugees. The British occupied the city until the war's end in 1783.

General George Washington returned in victory to New York. On December 4, 1783, he bade farewell to his officers by dining with them at Fraunces Tavern, on Pearl Street (see p 48). Washington was a natural choice as the new nation's first president; New York City became America's first capital, though only for a year.

The City Spreads

The city harbors a mixture of old and new architecture.

New York prospered as peace returned. By 1800 the population had reached 60,000, mostly crammed into a labyrinth of dirty,

narrow streets at the southern end of Manhattan Island. The city's grid plan, covering the whole of the island, was drawn up in 1811 and development began to move northward. A major boost came in 1825 with the opening of the 362mi Erie Canal from Buffalo to Albany. The waterway provided a trade route to the emergent Midwest. As railways developed, New York became the nation's major seaport and point of entry for immigrants from across the Atlantic.

The city began to grow upward in the late 1800s with the introduction of steel construction techniques and the development of the elevator. One of the first New York skyscrapers (then defined as any building over 10 floors), the Flatiron Building, appeared in 1902. In 1913 the 60-story Woolworth Building was trumpeted as the world's tallest at 792ft high. Since then a dozen New York skyscrapers have surpassed it, most recently Donald Trump's World Tower, at 881ft, the world's tallest residential building.

Immigration – The Huddled Masses

In the days when most people journeyed by sea, two landmarks greeted those arriving in New York. The first was the monumental Statue of

Left: The distinctive Flatiron Building was one of the first skyscrapers in New York.

The Statue of Liberty welcomed immigrants to their new home.

Liberty proclaiming "give me your tired, your poor, your huddled masses, yearning to breathe free." The second was fortress-like Ellis Island, through which all would-be immigrants had to pass as they underwent a succession of medical and document checks and interviews.

Between 1892 and 1954 about 12 million new Americans ran the Ellis Island gauntlet to create a new life in the land of their dreams. Many settled within a few miles of the island in one or another of the city's many ethnic neighborhoods. The first major

The Ellis Island Immigration Museum occupies the islet just north of the Statue of Liberty.

European groups to arrive were the Irish and the Germans. Driven abroad by the Great Potato Famine of 1846 and later disasters, the Irish soon constituted a quarter of the city's population.

The 1880s and 90s brought a flood of newcomers from Eastern Europe–Czechs, Poles, Lithuanians, and especially Jews from every part of the Russian Empire. There was a similar influx of Southern Italians. But be they tailors from the Warsaw ghetto or Sicilian peasants, a new ghetto awaited them in the squalid tenements and sweatshops of the Lower East Side.

Many of Chinatown's first residents had built the railroads in the West, only to flee a growing Anti-Chinese movement. Today Chinatown still serves as a hub for the city's Chinese population of 330,000.

Even as following generations left for the suburbs and farther, newcomers came to take their place. After World War II, blacks

Little Italy is one of the many ethnic areas in New York.

21

and Puerto Ricans came to the city by the hundreds of thousands. Many recent immigrants have come from the former Soviet Union, the Dominican Republic, and the Asian subcontinent.

THE PEOPLE AND CULTURE

New York City has often been called a melting pot, as each wave of immigrants strived to take its coveted place in the land of the free. The desire to assimilate did erode ethnic distinctions to some degree, but many of the people who settled in New York brought their culture with them and held to its values and customs as they underwent the metamorphosis that turned them into Americans. They lived within their own ethnic groups and spoke their native tongues. They worshipped in chapels, synagogues, mosques and temples like the ones they left behind, and celebrated the festivals of their old-world calendars.

Today New York is perhaps best described

News vendor in Chinatown.

as a mosaic, with many distinctly different, interlocking pieces. The pattern changes as one group moves on and another moves in. The original settlers – the Dutch and English – are now well dispersed, and the descendants of some of the earlier immigrants have left the city. There's still a few signs of the old German presence in Manhattan's Yorkville, but you'll have no difficulty finding the Irish in the Bronx and parts of Queens. Little Italy and nearby Chinatown are easily identifiable enclaves downtown. The Jews of Manhattan's Lower East Side moved on to the Bronx, Brooklyn and Queens. Their places were

New York's busy streets reflect the rich mixture of ethnic communities.

taken by Puerto Ricans who are now, in turn, being displaced by young artists and professionals. The three eras coexist, though, in the neighborhood's thriving commercial life. Other Caribbean and African-American communities can be found in Harlem, the Bronx, Brooklyn, the Upper West Side and lower Washington Heights.

The Cultural Scene

The most rewarding result of New York's ethnic mix is its rich and diverse culture. It is home to more art galleries, museums, concert halls and theaters than any other city in the US. There are about 40 Broadway theaters, with another 125 or so offering off-Broadway productions, mostly downtown. The city also offers about 125

Times Square anchors the Theater District.

movie theaters and 500 art galleries.

New York-inspired art, architecture, dance, drama, film, literature and music – be it hip-hop born on the streets of the Bronx, downtown punk or Broadway show tunes – has had an impact throughout the world.

Education has been a priority in New York since the days of Peter Stuyvesant. For more than a century New York residents did not have to pay for university tuition. Fees were imposed only in 1976 when the city was on the brink of bankruptcy. About 208,000 students are enrolled in the colleges of the City University of New York. And the New York Public Library, on Fifth Avenue, boasts more than 15 million items and is one of the largest research libraries in the world.

There's a real buzz around Times Square and Broadway at night.

MUST SEE

To obtain information on sightseeing services, maps and popular sights, stop at the Time Square Visitor Center (*open year-round daily 8am-8pm*), Broadway between 46th and 47th streets. The following is a selected list of attractions that no first-time visitor should miss. Each will be discussed in detail in this section.

American Museum of Natural History★★★ Dominating Central Park, between 77th and 81st streets, this world-famous museum celebrated its 125th anniversary in 1995. It numbers millions of objects in its collections.
Ellis Island★★ Millions of immigrants first set foot on US soil here. The **Ellis Island Immigration Museum★★** brings their experiences into sharp perspective.
Empire State Building★★★ Located on Fifth Avenue at 34th Street, this New York landmark was built in the early 1930s. The two observatories can be visited daily until midnight (last elevator goes up at 11:15pm).
Museum of Modern Art★★★ MoMA, whose collection of modern art is among the world's greatest, has moved to Queens during a three-year renovation to its Midtown building.
Metropolitan Museum of Art★★★ Set into Central Park along Fifth Avenue from 81st to 84th Street, this museum can hold your interest for days on end.
Rockefeller Center★★★ A shopping, entertainment and dining complex between Fifth and Sixth avenues and 47th and 52nd streets.
Central Park★★★ Set in the center of Manhattan, the park offers a tranquil retreat from the bustle of the city, with numerous recreation facilities as well as the Zoo, the

The gold statue of Prometheus presides over the Lower Plaza at Rockefeller Center.

Lake and Belvedere Castle to explore.

Statue of Liberty★★★ Still beckoning visitors, this gift from France, erected in 1886, commemorates the 1778 alliance between France and the US.

United Nations Building★★★ Be sure to take the tour of this 20C landmark, on First Avenue, between 42nd and 49th streets.

World Trade Center Site Since the towers fell, the site has become a place of pilgrimage for New Yorkers and visitors who want to reflect on the events of September 11, 2001, and remember the thousands who died that day.

INTRODUCING NEW YORK

The prospect of cramming as many of New York's famous sights as possible into one brief visit seems daunting, but a wide choice of organized tours can help any visitor become familiar with the Big Apple. Depending on your particular interests, your energy level and your budget, you can go sightseeing by helicopter or boat, by bus or limousine, or on foot. There are cultural tours, walking heritage tours of the Lower East Side (taking in Chinatown and Little Italy), bicycle tours of Central Park, gospel tours of Harlem… you name it, they've got it.

It can be bewildering to arrive in a big city where you don't know a soul and have no idea where to start your explorations; luckily New York has an organization to help – the **Big Apple Greeter** (☎ 212/669–8159). Greeters are enthusiastic New Yorkers who like to share their city with visitors and provide a helping hand ("We like to make the Big Apple feel smaller"). Your personal greeter will show you local haunts and how to use the subway. Your questions will be answered and you'll learn about the city's mainstream and offbeat attractions, as well as its gardens and quiet corners. The greeter service is free, but 48hrs' notice is advisable.

By Helicopter

Offering an overview of Manhattan, helicopter flights – from a 5min spin above Midtown or the New York Harbor to a 30min jaunt up the Hudson River Valley to see the autumn leaves – are unforgettable trips. **Liberty Helicopters** (☎ 212/967-6464) depart Midtown from the heliport at 12th Avenue and W. 30th Street daily, and from the Downtown heliport at Pier 6 Mon-Fri.

The Circle Line takes visitors around Manhattan Island.

By Boat

Passengers get a panoramic view of the Manhattan skyline with **Circle Line** (☎ 212/563–3200), whose vessels circumnavigate Manhattan Island in a 3hr, 35mi narrated tour.

Two-hour cruises around Lower Manhattan and out to the Statue of Liberty, and a Harbor Lights dusk cruise (7-9pm) are also available. The season is from mid-March through December. Reservations are advisable. Cruises depart from Pier 83, on 42nd Street at the Hudson River.

Spirit Cruises (☎ 212/727–2789) offer daily lunch and dinner cruises with a floor show and dance bands. **Gray Line** (☎ 212/397–2600) features a variety of Manhattan tours by bus, boat or helicopter.

On Foot

Below is a sampling of walking tours of
New York that introduce the visitor to
particular areas, famous sights and
attractions, or explore themes such as
architecture or history.

Adventure on a Shoestring
(☎ 212/265–2663)
Big Onion Tours
(☎ 212/439–1090)
Grand Tour of Midtown
(☎ 212/883-2420)
The Miracle of 34th Street
(☎ 212/868–0521)
Radical Walking Tours
(☎ 718/492–0069)
Lower East Side Tenement Tours
(☎ 212/431–0233 ext. 241)

*Signs, signs
everywhere.*

Special Interest Tours

The city also has a varied range of special
interest tours, which are often tailored to
special events at different times of the year.
For details of what is available during your
visit, check with the Times Square Visitors
Center *(46th and Broadway; open year round
daily 8am–8pm)*.

   A number of the city's major buildings and
complexes offer guided tours. A highly
recommended one is the 1hr behind-the-
scenes tour at Lincoln Center. The National
Broadcasting Company (NBC), at
Rockefeller Plaza, gives a tour every 15min
from 9:30am to 4:30pm. *(children under six
years are not permitted)*. Radio City Music Hall,
at 1260 Sixth Avenue (Avenue of the
Americas), offers a highly popular tour
lasting about one hour, during which visitors
get to meet one of the famous Rockettes.

MANHATTAN WALKS

The best way to get to know New York is by exploring the city on foot. Here are three suggested 2hr walks that give a taste of Manhattan.

Greenwich Village★★

New York's "Left Bank," the Village is an eccentric area of back streets, small shops, sidewalk cafés and both noisy and intimate bars. To get there, take the 1 or 9 train to Christopher Street/Sheridan Square. On arrival walk west on Christopher Street to Bleecker Street. Christopher Street, full of lively gay bars (which don't mind straight customers) was the scene of 1969 riots following a police raid on the Stonewall Inn at no. 51. This incident launched the Gay Liberation Movement.

Turn left on Bleecker Street, with its Italian

Street vendors line Prince Street in SoHo.

ambience, cross Seventh Avenue and continue to Sixth Avenue, where America's first saint, Mother Cabrini, worshipped at the Church of Our Lady of Pompeii.

At the corner of Bleecker and MacDougal streets stand two cafés whose names resounded in Beatnik times: the **Café Borgia**, previously The Scene, and Jack Kerouac's favorite, **Le Figaro Café**.

Heading north on MacDougal Street takes you past the **Provincetown Playhouse**, which saw the première productions of Eugene O'Neill's plays. MacDougal Street leads into the southwest corner of **Washington Square★★**, heart of the Village and the home at various times of writers Henry James, John Dos Passos, Theodore Dreiser and O. Henry.

Many of the buildings surrounding Washington Square are part of **New York University**. The Row, a group of Federal-style houses along Washington Square North, presides over the bustling, tree-shaded square frequented by rollerbladers, chess players and street entertainers. In May/June and September every year, hundreds of artists display their work as part of the **Washington Square Outdoor Art Exhibit**. **Washington Arch★**, commemorating the centennial of the inauguration of the first president of the US, marks the southern end of Fifth Avenue.

From Fifth Avenue, turn left onto W. 10th Street, where the **Church of the Ascension** features a superb mural by John LaFarge. Continue to Sixth Avenue, and follow Christopher Street back to Sheridan Square.

Chinatown★★
Crowded and noisy, New York's pulsating Chinatown is steadily expanding from its

A vegetable stall in Chinatown.

heart on Mott Street. Chinatown's side streets are well worth exploring. To get there take the 6, J, M, N, R, Q, W, or Z trains to Canal Street. Then, for an instant taste of Chinatown, walk east along Canal, with its shops and stalls selling fresh fish and exotic fruit and vegetables.

Turn right onto the Bowery and walk down to Confucius Plaza, distinguished by a bronze statue of the sage. Chatham Square is surrounded by buildings dating from the late 18C and early 19C. The First Shearith Israel cemetery on the south side of the square dates from 1683.

At the southwest corner of Chatham Square, turn right onto Mott Street, a vibrant, teeming thoroughfare crammed with Chinese and other Asian restaurants and shops. The Eastern States Buddhist Temple at no. 64 has been in existence for more than 80 years. If you continue north

Take a Saturday evening stroll through the busy streets of Chinatown, mingling with the shoppers stocking up in the colorful grocery stores, before stopping at the Peking Duck House, on Mott Street, to taste the best Peking duck in the city.

The entrance to the New York Stock Exchange.

on Mott Street, it will take you back to Canal Street.

Financial District★

Southern Manhattan is where fortunes and reputations are made and lost. Take the 4 or 5 train to **Wall Street★★**, a center of financial activity since 1792, when a group of stockbrokers met under a buttonwood tree and agreed to form the forerunner of the **New York Stock Exchange★** *(see p 52)*. Just across the street is **Federal Hall National Memorial**, the site of the nation's first capitol. George Washington was inaugurated here in 1789.

Look west along Wall Street for a superb view of **Trinity Church★★**, framed by skyscrapers. This was the city's tallest structure when it was built in 1846. About halfway down Wall Street – the entire thoroughfare is less than 600yds long – walk south on William Street and continue to Hanover Square, a placid oasis dotted with trees and benches. Captain Kidd once lived here, and the New York Cotton Exchange operated from the building now occupied by the famous bar **Harry's at Hanover Square**.

From the southeast corner of the square, walk south along Pearl Street to Broad Street. You will pass the Georgian Revival **Fraunces Tavern Museum★** *(see p 48)*. Here the entire block of houses is a listed historic district. Across the street, in the plaza at 85 Broad Street, you can peer through a glass panel to see the foundations of the 17C tavern that once served as City Hall.

After crossing Broad Street, head north and continue along Bridge Street, then turn right onto State Street. The ornate 1707 US Custom House, now home to the **National**

Trinity Church rises at the western end of Wall Street.

Museum of the American Indian★★, faces Bowling Green, the city's first public park when it opened in 1773.

From State Street, stroll through **Battery Park★**, to admire the view of New York Harbor and visit the **Castle Clinton National Monument★**, a brick fortress completed in 1811. Also here is the ticket office for ferries to Ellis Island and the Statue of Liberty. Go east through the park to the Staten Island Ferry terminal and the South Ferry subway station.

The American bald eagle forms the centerpiece of the East Coast Memorial in Battery Park.

ATTRACTIONS

It would be impossible to give a comprehensive listing of New York's many tourist
attractions. Instead, we offer a selection
from which you can design your own
itinerary. This detailed reference
concentrates on sights in Manhattan or
places easily accessible from there, and
highlights museums, churches, parks and
zoos, and sights of historical and general
interest. Later sections cover the other
boroughs and nearby areas located beyond
the city limits.

Museums

The **American Craft Museum★**, at 40 W.
53rd Street, is the exhibition center of the
American Craft Council. It shows off the
nation's best work in basketware, ceramics,
glass, wood, metal and textiles.

The **American Museum of the Moving
Image★**, off Steinway Street at 35th Avenue
and 36th Street in Queens, occupies part of
the former Astoria Film Studios, which
opened in 1917. The museum is a montage
of film, television and video history.
Memorabilia includes costumes and sets
from noted productions.

The **American Museum of Natural
History★★★**, at Central Park West between
77th and 81st streets, is the largest of its kind
in the world, with 30 million artifacts and
specimens. It has a huge collection of
dinosaurs, mammoths and a life-size model
whale. State-of-the-art dinosaur halls,
exhibiting the skeletons of *Tyrannosaurus
Rex* and *Apatosaurus*, are part of the $30
million restructuring of the fossil collection
which was completed in 1996. The six halls
demonstrate contemporaneous and

historical evolutionary relationships as well as the development of vertebrates using the world's most important array of fossils.

The Hall of Human Biology and Evolution explores human heritage through the latest multimedia technology. The newest addition to the first floor is the Hall of Biodiversity, which includes a walk-through diorama of an African rain forest. The Naturemax Theater features tours of the human body and the universe on a massive screen four floors high and 60ft wide.

Abutting the museum's north wall and looking out on 81st Street is the high-tech sphere-in-a-dome **Rose Center for Earth and Space.** Mysteries of the cosmos are revealed in the Hayden planetarium Space Theater. The Hall of Planet Earth focuses on our planet's geology and climate; the hall of the Universe features models of cosmic phenomena and interstellar artifacts.

The **Brooklyn Museum of Art★★**, on Eastern Parkway, is within easy reach of Manhattan; the Eastern Parkway subway station is right outside the museum's entrance. Its collections encompass over one and a half million objects, which range from Ancient Egyptian to contemporary American. Pre-Columbian, Oceanic, African, Chinese and Japanese art are all represented.

The outstanding Egyptian collection ranks among the finest in the world. It includes choice pieces from the Old Kingdom and from the much later Ptolemaic Period.

The fine assemblage of European and American paintings and sculptures features 58 works by Rodin as well as paintings by Homer, Copley, Sargent and Cassatt.

The **Children's Museum of Manhattan**, 212 W. 83rd Street, presents exhibits geared for kids and plenty of fascinating hands-on experiences. Children can use television cameras, draw cartoons and mess around with paint.

The **Ellis Island Immigration Museum**★★ celebrates the 12 million souls who disembarked at Ellis Island between 1892 and 1954. Through poignant photographs, memorabilia, film and tapes, you can appreciate the dreams and fears of the multitudes seeking a new life in the New World. The American Immigrant Wall of Honor is a 625ft double-sided semicircular wall, engraved with the names of nearly half a million immigrants. There is no charge to visit the museum. Ferries leave Battery Park on the half-hour Jun–Sept from 9:30am to 4:30pm; and until 3:30pm the rest of the year. The round-trip ferry fare includes the option to visit the Statue of Liberty.

Phillip Ratner's statue of James Pulitzer.

Below: Ellis and Liberty Islands.

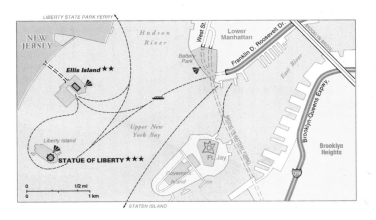

The Frick Collection★★★, at 1 E. 70th Street, is housed in the Beaux-Arts mansion built for steel magnate Henry Clay Frick. This gem of a museum features works by Rembrandt, Bellini and El Greco among its masterpieces. Visitors will find the marble Garden Court, with its long, shallow pool, a restful retreat.

The **Solomon R. Guggenheim Museum★★**, on Fifth Avenue at 89th Street, was designed by Frank Lloyd Wright. This spiral-shaped building is a work of art in itself. Opened in 1959, and since extended, it displays modern art by such masters as Chagall, Klee and Picasso.

The Jewish Museum★★, on Fifth Avenue at 94th Street, holds 28,000 international examples of Jewish ceremonial and other objects, making it one of the largest of such collections in the western hemisphere. Much of the collection consists of pieces saved from synagogues as the Nazis swept across Europe at the start of World War II.

An interior view of the Solomon R. Guggenheim Museum.

Exhibitions portray Jewish life throughout history and a special focus is placed on the poverty of the early Lower East Side immigrants and the sufferings endured during the Holocaust.

The Metropolitan Museum of Art★★★ (MMA) (Fifth Ave. at 82nd Street ☎ 212/879-5500) is an absolute must on anyone's tour of New York.

The MMA covers four blocks and its three floors cover a total area of 46 acres. It houses more than two million objects, of which only one-quarter are on exhibit. Not surprisingly, this is the largest art museum in the western world. The MMA opened in 1872. A collection of 143 Dutch and Flemish paintings were donated in 1877. Its renowned antiquities collection started with a single Roman sarcophagus, followed by the acquisition of 6,000 objects from a general who had served as the US consul in Cyprus. Today, you would need to set aside several days to view everything on show. The best way to tackle the MMA is to work out a strategy based on your particular interests, and make sure you are wearing comfortable shoes. From the main entrance on Fifth Avenue, you enter the Great Hall. Pick up floor plans or recorded tours at the information desk *(some galleries may be closed)*.

The museum houses works of art from ancient civilizations to the present day, including hundreds of world-renowned masterpieces. Permanent displays feature tapestries, musical instruments, costumes and ornaments. The MMA's major collections are European Art, American Art, Egyptian Antiquities, Arts of Africa, Oceania and the Americas, Asian and Medieval Art.

The **European Gallery★★★** features classics

by Breugel, Van Eyck, Van Gogh and Velazquez. The **American Wing★★★** contains a living room designed by Frank Lloyd Wright. On the roof of the MMA is a **garden of contemporary sculpture**, open in the summer. The **Egyptian Wing** spans several thousand years of Egyptian civilization. A central green carpet flanked by marble floors evokes the Nile with deserts on either side. One dramatic glass-walled gallery houses the small 1C BC **Temple of Dendur**, a gift from the Egyptian government.

The museum's one-day admission charge also covers **The Cloisters★★★**. This stunning re-creation, overlooking the Hudson River in Fort Tryon Park, incorporates parts of five French medieval cloisters brought to the US. The Cloisters contains much of the MMA's medieval collection. It can be reached by car

The entrance to the Metropolitan Museum of Art.

or public transportation.

The **Museum of the City of New York★★**, 1220 Fifth Avenue at 103rd Street, is a useful source of information on the city. A major feature is Big Apple, a multimedia presentation on the city's history from 1524 to the present. Period alcoves dating from the 17C to around 1900 are also on display along with three centuries of silver. Don't miss the prized collection of dollhouses. The museum launched Project September 11 to collect material that document or relate to the events of that day.

A Magnolia Vase by Tiffany and Co., dating from 1893.

The **Museum of Modern Art★★★ (MoMA)** owns an unsurpassed collection of modern art – 100,000 pieces ranging from post-Impressionism to Pop Art. Its Midtown building, undergoing a major expansion, reopens in 2005. Until then selections from its permanent collection and special exhibitions will be shown at the MoMA QNS, at 33rd Street and Queens Boulevard, a few stops from Midtown by the 7 train.

The **Museum of Television and Radio★**, at 25 W. 52nd Street between Fifth and Sixth avenues, allows visitors to monitor any of the programs in its vast collection on individual TV and radio consoles. Drama, news items, commercials and documentaries are included in the museum's archives.

The **New York Historical Society★★**, on Central Park West and 77th Street, is the city's oldest museum. The society's new Luce Center displays its nearly 40,000 objects to the public in a "working storage" format. Its permanent collection of 2,500 paintings includes notable examples from the Hudson River school.

The **New York Transit Museum**, in Brooklyn at Boerum Place and Schermerhorn Street (☎ 718/694-5100), is suitably sited in a former 1930s subway station. It features restored subway cars and displays transit objects and memorabilia covering an 80-year period.

Isamu Noguchi Garden Museum★★, at 32-37 Vernon Boulevard in Queens, features sculptures by the late Japanese-American artist. The Garden museum, designed by Noguchi on the site of his former studio, is closed for renovations. Until August 2003, the collection is located at 36-01 43rd Avenue, just blocks from MoMA QNS.

The **Queens Museum of Art**, at Flushing Meadows-Corona Park, was built as the New York Pavilion for the 1939 World's Fair. The museum is noted for its continually updated, large-scale model of the five boroughs.

The **Whitney Museum of American Art**★★, located at 945 Madison Avenue at 75th Street, was founded in Greenwich Village in 1931 by the sculptor Gertrude Vanderbilt Whitney. Major 20C artists featured in its collection include Alexander Calder, Jackson Pollock and Andy Warhol.

Churches

Places of worship in New York City can be counted by the thousands; just about every religious faith is represented among the city's population of 8 million.

Roman Catholics form one of the largest groups. The majority of priests are of Irish descent, but since the city's Catholics come

The facade of neo-Gothic Saint Patrick's Cathedral.

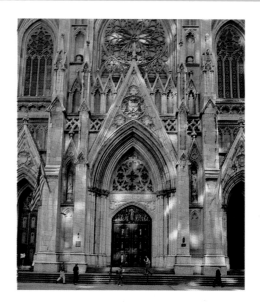

from all over the world, services are held in about two dozen languages.

Exuberant black gospel services intrigue visitors so much that the gospel tour has become a regular feature in Harlem.

New York is home to one of the world's largest Jewish communities. Half the city's synagogues are in Brooklyn.

One of the city's great cathedrals is the Roman Catholic **Saint Patrick's Cathedral★★**, at Fifth Avenue and 50th Street. This Gothic Revival cathedral took just over a quarter of a century to build and was consecrated in 1879. Saint Patrick's is open daily from 7am to 6pm; guided tours are available.

Hailed as the world's largest cathedral built in the Gothic style, the **Cathedral of St.**

John the Divine★★, at 112th Street and Amsterdam Avenue, boasts an interior longer than two football fields. It features some exquisite stained glass. Construction began in 1892 and, over a century later, the cathedral is still a work in progress. Tours are given daily (except Monday) at 11am, and Sunday at 1pm.

Trinity Church★★ offers a haven on Broadway at Wall Street. The 1846 Episcopal church's 280ft spire made it New York's tallest building until its title was usurped in the skyscraper age. It is the third church on the site, its charter dating from 1697.

St. Paul's Chapel★★, on Broadway at Fulton Street, built in 1766, is the oldest church in Manhattan. George Washington worshipped here during his presidency – his pew can still be seen.

Sights of Historical or General Interest

Carnegie Hall★, at 156 W. 57th Street, opened in 1891. Performers as diverse as Tchaikovsky and the Beatles have drawn crowds here, and it is still hailed as having the best acoustics of any concert hall in the world. The **Chrysler Building★★★**, on Lexington Avenue at 42nd Street, has a special place in the hearts of New Yorkers. This Art Deco skyscraper, crowned by its distinctive spire of stainless steel, houses offices and a lobby decked with walls of African marble and elevator doors of inlaid wood.

City Hall★★, at Broadway and Murray Street, has been the seat of New York City government since 1812. *(City Hall is only accessible to the public through group tours.)*

Its extravagant ArtDeco design makes the Chrysler Building a favorite with New Yorkers.

The **Empire State Building★★★**, at 34th Street and Fifth Avenue, was built in the Art Deco style in 1931 and became the world's tallest skyscraper – 1,454ft high. Today, it ranks as the second tallest in the US behind the Sears Tower. Two observatories offer superb views of the city, an enclosed one on the 102nd floor and an outdoor one on the 86th floor.

Also exciting is **Skyride**, introduced in 1995, a thrilling simulated trip to Manhattan landmarks, such as Central Park, Times Square and the FAO Schwarz toy store. The ride is offered as part of a joint discount ticket to visitors going to the top of the Empire State Building.

Fraunces Tavern★, 54 Pearl Street at Broad Street, is the establishment where George Washington held his farewell dinner after the Revolutionary War. On the upper floors, exhibits outline New York's role in the war and explain how the city became the temporary seat of the federal government.

Gracie Mansion★, on East End Avenue, is the official residence of the Mayor of New York. A Federal-style building overlooking the East River from Carl Schurz Park, the mansion was originally built for a wealthy merchant in 1799.

Grand Central Terminal★★, 42nd Street and Park Avenue, is one of the few railroad stations in the world to be declared a national landmark. Opened in 1913 and recently extensively renovated, this Beaux-Arts terminal features a massive main concourse – 375ft long with a 125ft–high vaulted ceiling, originally decorated with 2,500 painted stars. Free lunchtime guided tours by the Municipal Arts Society begin at the information booth in the main

The mighty Empire State Building, seen from Macy's Department store.

concourse (12:30pm Wednesdays).

The **Intrepid Sea-Air-Space Museum** is docked in the Hudson River at Pier 86, W. 46th Street. Here, the 910ft–long aircraft carrier *Intrepid*, serves as a technology museum showcasing naval, aviation and aerospace achievements.

Lincoln Center for the Performing Arts, on Broadway from 62nd to 66th streets, New York's premier performing arts venue, encompasses a 15-acre complex of halls; the three largest are grouped around a fountain on a wide plaza.

The glass-fronted **Metropolitan Opera House**, set farthest back, is the focal point of this group. The visitor's eyes are immediately drawn to the huge Chagall murals clearly visible from the outside. Here, lavish productions take place on a stage the size of a football field. The opera house is flanked on the left by the New York State

Grand Central Terminal bustles at rush hour.

Theater, home to the New York City Ballet, and on the right by Avery Fisher, where the New York Philharmonic performs. Lincoln Center comprises five major theater buildings, 12 resident companies, the New York Public Library for the Performing Arts, and the famous Julliard School.

Madison Square Garden occupies the space above Pennsylvania Station, between 31st and 33rd streets at Seventh Avenue. It claims to be "the world's most famous arena." Seating more than 20,000 spectators, it is the home of the New York Knicks and the New York Rangers, who, respectively, play basketball and ice hockey here from October to April. Concerts and other events take place throughout the year.

The **New York Stock Exchange★**, 20 Broad Street, allows visitors to view the trading floor. When you're on vacation, it can be gratifying to watch other people working,

Lincoln Center shines at Christmastime.

Frenzied activity at the New York Stock Exchange.

and they do it frenziedly here. The show is free – just pick up a ticket at the building's entrance. *(As a security precaution, the exchange has been closed to visitors.)*

Rockefeller Center★★★ is a vast office, shopping, dining and entertainment complex between Fifth and Sixth avenues and 48th and 51st streets. Pick up a map of the area in the lobby of the 70-floor **GE Building★★**, the center's highest skyscraper, to take a self-guided tour.

On the Lower Plaza stands the famous statue of Prometheus. There's outdoor dining here in summer, while in winter the area is transformed into a skating rink. Rockefeller Center boasts more than 30 restaurants, including the legendary Rainbow Room on the 65th floor of the GE Building, and the Fashion Café, owned by Naomi Campbell, Elle MacPherson and Claudia Schiffer.

Theodore Roosevelt Birthplace National Historic Site★ is located at 28 East 20th Street

*Ice skating at
Rockefeller Center.*

*Rockefeller Center's
statue of Atlas on
Fifth Avenue.*

at Fifth Avenue. The only US president to be born in New York, Roosevelt lived in this 19C brownstone until he was 14. Now restored, the building contains personal mementoes of his presidency and also of his adventures as a soldier and game hunter.

The **South Street Seaport Historic District**★★ covers 11 square blocks along the East River south of the Brooklyn Bridge. The Seaport Visitor Center, which is the main entrance to Seaport, is at 12-14 Fulton Street. New York has made the most of this East River landmark district, which was a busy seaport in the early 19C. Today, the restored area features historic vessels, boutiques, antique shops, street performers, the **South Street Seaport Museum** and its highlight, the four-masted tall ship, *Peking*. A number of other historic ships can be visited at Piers 15 and 16. They include the schooner *Pioneer*, built more than 100 years ago, and a 1925 steam ferry. The *Pioneer* offers two-hour tours around the harbor under sail.

The **Staten Island Ferry**★ is one of the most famous features of New York life, taking visitors to Staten Island and back to Battery Park (State St.). The ferry doesn't stop at the Statue of Liberty, but it provides a good view of it – along with splendid views of the city itself. The trip lasts about 25min each way.

The **Statue of Liberty**★★★, reaches 305ft in the air with her torch. An observation deck on the 10th floor affords spectacular **views**★★★ of New York and the harbor. Another 162 steps along a narrow, circular staircase take you to her crown. The ferry trip from Battery Park to the statue takes about 15min. (*As a security precaution, the*

Feel the exhilaration of a windy voyage aboard the famed Staten Island ferry as it plies the waters of New York Harbor.

South Street
Seaport's Pier 17.

*statue itself remains closed, although Liberty
Island is still open to visitors.)*

United Nations Headquarters★★★, at First
Avenue and 43rd Street, includes the
General Assembly Building, with its
2,000–seat hall. Be sure to note the position
of the great pendulum in the visitor center
lobby when you go in, and see how far it has
moved by the time you come out. Daily tours

55

leave every half hour between 9:30am and 4:45pm.

The **Vietnam Veterans Memorial**, on Water Street in the Financial District, consists of a granite and glass wall, 66ft long, etched with extracts from diaries and letters written by American troops during the war.

The **Woolworth Building**★★★ stood as the world's tallest building from its opening in 1913 until 1930. Located on

The United Nations building.

Broadway at Park Place, the 60-floor Gothic-style "Cathedral of Commerce," housed the headquarters of the Woolworth Corporation. The 3-story-high **lobby**, a design masterpiece, features a barrel-vaulted ceiling above golden marble walls and glass mosaics. Bas-relief caricatures in the lobby depict Frank Woolworth himself counting out nickels and dimes (no doubt to symbolize his famous "5 &10" stores); the architect, Cass Gilbert, holding a model of the building; and the renting agent carrying out business.

Experience the unforgettable first close-up sight of the Statue of Liberty as the Battery Park ferry approaches Liberty Island.

The Woolworth Building was once the world's tallest (right).

Cleanup of the 16-acre **World Trade Center** site began immediately after its destruction on September 11; that work was finished in May 2002. The 1,350ft Twin Towers anchored a 16-acre, seven-building complex. Workers removed 1.5 million tons of steel and debris even as they continued to search for remains of the 2,797 who died. A viewing wall has been erected along Church Street. A number of displays mounted along the wall trace the history of the site, in text, photos and maps, from the era before the World Trade Center through its construction to the future for the site.

That future remains very much undecided. A memorial and an integrated Downtown transit hub are sure to be built (work on a new PATH commuter rail terminal in the sublevels of the site is already underway).

Just across West Street from the site is the **World Financial Center** office complex, now recovered from the damage it suffered on 9/11. Much of the 120ft-high glass-and-steel **Winter Garden★**, nestled between the WFC towers, was destroyed by falling debris. During a restoration completed on the one-year anniversary of the attack, workers replaced 2,000 broken panes of glass and relaid 1.2 million pounds of Italian marble. **Battery Park City** – begun in the 1960s on the landfill created by the original excavation of the WTC site and now home to more than 30,000 people – has also cleaned up. A new Ritz-Carlton hotel opened in early 2002 and new residential construction has resumed.

Pause to remember the 2,797 lives that were lost when the Twin Towers fell on the morning of September 11, 2001.

Parks and Zoos

Battery Park★, so called because of the battery of cannons pointing out to sea, is a pleasant expanse of statues and greenery with a view of New York Harbor, Staten Island and the Statue of Liberty. On its grounds stands **Castle Clinton National Monument★**, built in the early 1800s to defend the city against the British. This fort now houses a museum illustrating its history. A kiosk there sells ferry tickets to Ellis Island and the Statue of Liberty.

The **Bronx Zoo★★★**, at Bronx River Parkway and Fordham Road, encompasses 265 acres of woodland, with the Bronx River running through it. The zoo houses over 700 species in habitats such as Himalayan Highlands, the World of Birds, Wild Asia and the new Congo Gorilla Forest and Wolf Woods. Much of the zoo can be viewed from the Skyfari cable car and the Bengali Express monorail. A 3-acre **children's zoo** showcases over 100 animals in

Damaged by falling debris on 9/11, Sphere, by Fritz Koenig, now stands in Battery Park.

their natural habitats.

The **New York Botanical Garden★★**, on Kazimiroff Boulevard, lies just across Fordham Road. Covering 250 acres, it contains 48 gardens and plant collections, the **Enid A. Haupt Conservatory ★★** and walking trails. Highlights include the Rose Garden, the Rhododendron Garden and **Everett Children's Adventure Garden**. In May 2002, the garden opened its new International Plant Science Center. The $100 million facility houses a research collection of 7 million plant specimens.

Brooklyn Botanic Garden★★, located on Washington Avenue, is noted for its extensive rose garden, springtime cherry

Roses color the Brooklyn Botanic Garden.

blossoms and a new tropical and desert plants conservatory. The **Discovery Garden** offers children a new slant on nature through imaginative exhibits.

Central Park offers activities for everyone.

Central Park★★★ covers 843 acres and stretches between 59th and 110th streets. It was designed by Frederick Law Olmsted and Calvert Vaux, who engineered a Romantic-era re-creation of nature that is very much man made. Roads, for instance, are deftly laid under the park's network of footpaths so traffic can pass through without disturbing the peace.

Work on the park began in 1857 and took 19 years to complete. The park is widely used throughout the year. Although the park is open until 1am, visitors should avoid secluded areas of the park after dark. Summer visitors enjoy picnicking, boating, cycling, roller-skating, horseback riding and kite-flying. Winter brings out the skaters, and if there's enough snow the skiers and sledders. The **Central Park Zoo★**, near the 64th Street entrance on Fifth Avenue, houses over 1,400 animals.

Open-air **Delacorte Theater** provides a venue for free performances of Shakespeare throughout the summer. Vaux designed nearby **Belvedere Castle** as an imitation Medieval Scottish castle. **Strawberry Fields**, near the park's W. 72nd Street entrance, is a hillside garden dedicated to the memory of John Lennon, who was murdered outside The Dakota, across the street. The best places for

The Boathouse Visitor Center in Brooklyn's Prospect Park occupies a former boathouse constructed in 1905 and modeled after a 16C Venetian building.

picnics are the Great Lawn and the Sheep Meadow, where a flock grazed until 1934.

On Saturdays during the summer, there are storytelling sessions (at 11am) for children at the statue of Hans Christian Andersen, near the model sailboat lake (just north of the E. 72nd Street entrance).

Maps and other information on Central Park are available at the Visitor Information Center located in the **Dairy** – milk was actually processed here at one time – between the zoo and the carousel.

Flushing Meadows-Corona Park, in Queens (easily accessible by subway), is the home of the **USTA National Tennis Center**, where the US Open is held *(see p 107)*. This was also the site of the 1939 and 1964 World's Fairs (some pavilions remain– notably the park's focal point, the 120ft-high Unisphere built by US Steel). The park offers activities from ice-skating to cycling, and a model airplane field. It also encompasses a children's farm, a zoo, the New York Hall of Science *(see p 70)*, and the Queens Museum of Art *(see p 44)*.

Pelham Bay Park, in the Bronx, is the largest park in the city, covering some 2,000 acres. It provides 1mi of beach and facilities for horseback riding, golf, cycling, fishing, tennis and picnicking.

Prospect Park★, in Brooklyn, is the pride of the borough. With more than 500 acres, it is an idyllic oasis of woods, meadowland, lakes and streams designed by Central Park's architects Olmsted and Vaux. Grand Army Plaza, at the park's entrance, is dominated by the **Soldiers' and Sailors' Memorial Arch**, modeled on the Arc de Triomphe in Paris. It pays homage to those who died in the Civil War.

Van Cortlandt Park, in the Bronx, provides a whole range of leisure activities, including golfing, boating and tennis. The antebellum **Van Cortlandt House Museum★** lies within the park.

The Queensboro Bridge links Manhattan to Queens and Brooklyn.

BEYOND MANHATTAN

New York City's wealth of sights include many found in the other boroughs. A number of major attractions were already described in the **Museums** and **General**

Interest sections *(these are cross-referenced in this section)*, but here is a breakdown of the rest of the city.

The Bronx

Apart from **Yankee Stadium★**, we advise you to avoid the poverty-stricken South Bronx.

The Bronx Zoo and New York Botanical Garden★★ *See p 60.*

City Island This small island offers a fishing-village ambience on Manhattan's doorstep, with boatbuilding, a yachting community, a nautical museum and seafood restaurants.

Pelham Bay Park *See p 64.*

Poe Cottage Poet and author Edgar Allan Poe spent his last years here, at East Kingsbridge and Grand Concourse, looking after his consumptive wife. Among other poems, he wrote *Annabel Lee* here.

Valentine-Varian House This farmhouse, on 3266 Bainbridge Avenue at E. 208th Street, was built by a blacksmith in 1758 and contains the Museum of Bronx History.

Van Cortlandt Park *See p 64.*

Wave Hill★ Theodore Roosevelt, Arturo Toscanini and Mark Twain have each made their home in the 1843 mansion located on this 28-acre estate, at 625 W. 252nd Street. A popular destination for New Yorkers on a day out, the estate comprises gardens, greenhouses, meadows and woodlands.

Woodlawn Cemetery This is the final resting place of many famous Americans, including Duke Ellington and F.W. Woolworth. Find out who's buried where from a leaflet available at the cemetery office.

Yankee Stadium★ "The House that Ruth Built," at 161st Street and River Avenue, is

America's most storied baseball field and home of the New York Yankees.

The Brooklyn and Manhattan bridges span the East River.

Brooklyn

Numerous ethnic groups, 19C architecture and a range of good restaurants, most of them considerably cheaper than those in Manhattan, make Brooklyn a worthwhile place to visit. The Brooklyn Bridge is the most famous means of access, with its pedestrian walkway spanning the East River above the vehicular lanes. Two other bridges, the Williamsburg and Manhattan, also provide links with Brooklyn. The Brooklyn-Battery Tunnel serves cars, and the subway provides easy access.

Atlantic Avenue This bustling street is home to one of the largest Middle Eastern communities in the US. Restaurants serving couscous and kebabs, and small antique shops all appeal to tourists.

A typical row of 19C brownstones in Brooklyn.

Brooklyn Academy of Music★ BAM, as it is called, at 30 Lafayette Avenue, is said to be the oldest continuously operating performing arts center in the US, founded in 1859. It has become New York's premier venue for avant-garde dance, drama, and music performance. In 1998 BAM opened the four-screen Rose Cinemas.

Brooklyn Heights Historic District★★ Federal-style and Greek Revival brownstones have been carefully restored in this 40-block tract of mainly 19C buildings. Prowl its quaint streets and enjoy the spectacular view of Manhattan from the Esplanade, overlooking the East River.

Brooklyn Historical Society The society's museum and library make up the most comprehensive collection of Brooklyn-related materials. Its landmark 1881 Queen Anne-style building on Pierrepont Street is scheduled to reopen after a 3-year renovation in spring 2003.

Brooklyn Botanic Garden★★ *See p 61.*
Brooklyn Museum★★ *See p 38.*
Coney Island *See p 72.*
Lefferts Homestead Built in 1776, this Dutch Colonial farmhouse in **Prospect Park**★ *(see p 64)* is now a children's museum.
New York City Transit Museum *See p 44.*
Plymouth Church of the Pilgrims Henry Ward Beecher led his campaign against slavery from this simple church on Orange Street in the Brooklyn Heights Historic District. The church was part of the Underground Railroad, a route along which slaves from the South were smuggled to freedom before the Civil War. Worshippers here included Abraham Lincoln and Mark Twain.

Queens

New York's largest borough, home to 167 nationalities, has become America's most diverse county. Astoria is home to the largest Greek population outside Greece; Forest Hills hosts the Russian Jewish quarter; Jackson Heights boasts Latin Americans and Indians; Flushing is known as Little Asia; and Corona Avenue is a Latin American enclave. Many African-American professionals live in Jamaica.

John F. Kennedy and La Guardia airports are also located in Queens.

American Museum of the Moving Image★
See p 37.

Bowne House The 1661 home of Quaker John Bowne, who won his fight for religious freedom under Dutch rule, is now a museum.

Flushing Meadows-Corona Park *See p 64.*

Isamu Noguchi Garden Museum★★ *See p 44.*

Jamaica Center for Arts and Learning The 1898 Italian Renaissance Revival building, at 161-04 Jamaica Avenue, houses a center for multi-ethnic performing and visual arts.

Jamaica Bay Wildlife Refuge Some 300 species of birds and other wildlife may be observed during nature walks in this large coastal reserve.

Kingsland Homestead Built c.1785 and administered by the Queens Historical Society, this ancient farm is situated at 143-35 37th Street.

New York Hall of Science Located in Flushing Meadows-Corona Park *(see p 64)*, this structure was erected for the 1964 World's Fair. Next to its striking building, construction has begun on Science City, which will double the hall's exhibition space when completed in 2004.

Queens Museum of Art *See p 44.*

Staten Island

Despite a rise in residential development since the opening in 1964 of the Verrazano-Narrows Bridge, Staten Island still contains a mostly rural interior. The best way to get to the borough is on the Staten Island Ferry.

Alice Austen House Museum★ A unique collection of photographs of New York Harbor, taken by Alice Austen over a period of more than 70 years, is housed in her cottage overlooking the Harbor.

Conference House This 1675 fieldstone manor house, at 7455 Hylan Boulevard, was the scene of abortive peace talks between Benjamin Franklin, John Adams and British Admiral Lord Howe in the early stages of the Revolutionary War. Today it houses an historical museum.

Historic Richmond Town★ Allow several hours for this collection of more than two dozen reconstructed buildings. Voorlezer's House is the oldest surviving elementary school in the country, built under the British administration in 1695. A museum, headquarters of the Staten Island Historical Society, traces three centuries of island life. Costumed guides chat with visitors, while others re-enact chores and demonstrate traditional crafts. Special events are staged throughout the year. The site can be easily reached by bus from the ferry terminal.

Jacques Marchais Center of Tibetan Art★ A rare collection of Tibetan arts and objects is displayed in this reproduction Buddhist temple, at 338 Lighthouse Avenue. Festivals are staged here occasionally by saffron-robed monks.

Snug Harbor Cultural Center Nearly 30 buildings covering various periods of American architecture stand in an 80-acre park, at 1000 Richmond Terrace. Originally a hospital and home for retired seamen, the grand buildings have been a city cultural center since 1976. Performances of opera, classical music and jazz as well as exhibitions of painting, sculpture and photography regularly take place here.

William T. Davis Wildlife Refuge A range of mammals, birds and reptiles, as well as plantlife, can be seen in the 260 acres of mixed habitats: tidal marsh, meadowlands, woods and freshwater wetlands.

FAMILY OUTINGS

New York features numerous opportunities for family outings. Here are just a few suggestions:

American Museum of Natural History★★★ *See p 37.*
Bronx Zoo★★★ *See p 60.*
Central Park★★★ *See p 62.*
Children's Museum of Manhattan *See p 39.*
Coney Island, in Brooklyn, is often overlooked, although it features a number of fun attractions: **Astroland**, an amusement park, boasts the white-knuckle Cyclone roller coaster and sideshows. The **New York Aquarium**★★ is home to thousands of exotic fish as well as performing sea lions, dolphins and beluga whales.

The **Discovery Garden** *See p 62.*
The Enchanted Forest, at 85 Mercer Street in SoHo, is an evocative shop with handmade toys and children's crafts and books.

FAO Schwarz, 767 Fifth Avenue at 58th Street, is a toy store founded in 1862 with the child in mind. The store offers an unbelievable selection of toys and games, and the staff wear costumes.

Intrepid Sea-Air-Space Museum, *See p 50.*

The **Roosevelt Island Tramway**, affords a wonderful skyline view as it crosses the East River from Manhattan to the sausage-shaped Roosevelt Island off the Upper East Side. The Manhattan tramport is at 60th Street

Wollman Ice-Skating Rink provides winter fun in southern Central Park.

and Second Avenue. The tramway's red cable cars have appeared in numerous movies, including *King Kong* and *Spider-Man*.

South Street Seaport Historic District★★
See p 54.

AWAY FROM IT ALL

Sometimes it's good to get out of the city.
You may want to see something of the areas
surrounding New York, or take a break from
city sightseeing. Here we give a selection of
beaches – the New Yorker's escape from the
end of May to the beginning of September –
and places to visit beyond the city limits.

On the Beach

It's easy to go to a beach from Manhattan.
Most of the nearer ones can be reached by
subway, but they get very crowded on
summer weekends. Brooklyn's **Coney Island
Beach**, probably the best known, became
prominent in the 1840s and was fashionable
for decades. Since the 1950s, however, it has
been in decline. The roller coaster and
other rides have a rather tired look and
there is a seedy air about the stalls and
sideshows; however, the 3.5mi beach is still
pleasant, the boardwalk provides an
enjoyable stroll and vendors serve the
traditional hot dogs.

Brighton Beach is along the same stretch
of Coney Island coast, but because of silting
the island is now actually a peninsula. Some
30,000 Russians have settled in the
neighborhood since the 1970s. Today you
can buy Russian dolls, drink vodka, eat blinis
and listen to the music of the balalaika and
accordion in the area New Yorkers call
"Little Odessa."

Another popular beach accessible by
subway is **Rockaway Beach★**, in Queens, with
more than 7mi of sand and surf occupying a
narrow spit of land between the Atlantic
Ocean and Jamaica Bay.

Beyond the eastern reaches of the city,
Long Island★★ offers miles of excellent

The boardwalk at Coney Island features the old-fashioned Cyclone roller coaster.

beaches with boardwalks, beach trails, restaurants and picnic areas. Many of the beaches, including **Long Beach** and **Jones Beach State Park★★**, can be reached by trains that run frequently from Manhattan's Penn Station. Set in a 2,400-acre park, Jones Beach boasts a 6.5mi stretch of sand and a 2mi boardwalk. Facilities include pools, golf courses and playgrounds. Outdoor concerts are popular in summer.

Some Long Island beaches are open only to local residents, but most – including ten in state parks – welcome everyone. Parking or entrance fees are charged during the summer.

One of New York's more famous beaches is **Fire Island★**. It contains 1,400 acres of **National Seashore★**, and is 32mi long but only .5mi wide at its widest point. Only local service vehicles are allowed. The island is accessible by ferry. The western end of the island has been designated **Robert Moses State Park★**. It is

connected by a causeway to the rest of Long Island, and so is accessible by car; buses also run during the summer from Port Authority Terminal (leaving early in the morning and returning late afternoon). This beach is an area of sand dunes with virtually no shade, but is pleasant and clean. The dunes offer sanctuary to seabirds and waterfowl.

The lighthouse at Montauk Point, Long Island.

Out of Town

The greater metropolitan area has plenty of places to choose from if you want to take a break of two or three days – or even just a day trip – out of the city. There are good rail and bus connections to Long Island and Connecticut, and to the near north lies the lovely countryside of the Hudson River Valley.

If you feel like going farther afield, Boston, Massachusetts, lies only 215mi to the north, while Niagara Falls, 450mi away by car, is not much more than an hour's trip by plane.

Long Island★★ Bordering the city on the east, Long Island has always been a popular hideaway for New Yorkers. Indeed, many of those who work in the city commute from homes on the island, which has excellent rail service running to Penn Station. The trip from Midtown Manhattan to the Long Island boundary is just 15mi, and from there to Montauk, at the island's tip, another 118mi *(about a 3hr drive)*. Within its sand-fringed shores, the island encompasses attractive rustic scenery and a host of quaint villages, many dating from the mid-17C.

At its eastern end the island splits into North Fork and South Fork, both served by rail. North Fork has fewer communities and a wilder landscape. There's a **state park** at **Orient Point** where you can also get a car ferry to New London, Connecticut. South Fork is home to the **Hamptons★★**, three small summer communities of wealthy residents, as well as Amagansett and the former whaling port of **Sag Harbor★**.

Long Island offers plenty to those who like the outdoors. From Montauk, on the eastern tip of South Fork, you can enjoy **whale-watching cruises**, seal cruises and seal walks, as well as horseback riding on the beach. Watersports enthusiasts can indulge in canoeing, kayaking, sailing, windsurfing, jet skiing, scuba diving and snorkeling. You can go deep-sea fishing on chartered craft from harbors on both shores.

For history buffs there are **whaling museums** at Cold Spring Harbor and Sag Harbor, the **Vanderbilt Museum★** at Centerport, the **Cradle of Aviation Museum** in Garden City, and the **Walt Whitman Birthplace State Historic Site** at Huntington. **Sagamore Hill National Historical Site★** at Oyster Bay is the restored country home of President Theodore Roosevelt. **Stony Brook★★**, on the North Shore, allows you to enjoy a Federal-style village of the 18C and 19C. A number of museums on the site enrich the experience. At **Old Bethpage**

There is plenty to see at the Old Bethpage Restoration Village on Long Island.

Restoration Village★★ you can see a farming community functioning as it would have done before the Civil War. Twenty-five historic buildings have been relocated here, and traditional crafts are demonstrated.

Revisit the Roaring Twenties at one of the dozen or so **Gold Coast mansions** (North Shore) that are open to the public. Fronting on Long Island Sound, these were the homes of the fabulously wealthy whose lifestyle was described by F. Scott Fitzgerald in *The Great Gatsby*.

Hudson River Valley★★★ New York City is soon left behind as you follow the Hudson River north – whether by car, train, bus, or on the river itself with the Hudson River Day Line ferry services.

Only 20mi from Midtown Manhattan is **Tarrytown**, the inspiration for Washington Irving's *Legend of Sleepy Hollow*. The creator of Rip Van Winkle made his home here at **Sunnyside★**, now a charming riverside estate museum open to the public.

Nearby are **Lyndhurst★**, a Gothic Revival mansion affording stunning views of the Hudson, and **Philipsburg Manor★**, built by Dutch settlers in the 17C.

Hyde Park, farther north just above Poughkeepsie, is the birthplace of Franklin D. Roosevelt, and has been designated a **National Historic Site★★**. Exhibitions recall the life of FDR and his family. He and his wife, Eleanor, a prominent international figure in her own right, are buried in the rose garden at Hyde Park. On the other side of the river, traveling south, is **West Point★★**, home of the US Military Academy. The academy is open to the public daily and has a visitor center and a **museum★★**.

WEATHER

New York enjoys a temperate climate, with four distinct seasons, ranging from bitterly cold winters to very hot summers. The best times to visit are spring and autumn when temperatures are at their most moderate. Even then there can be periods of torrential rain, and the pollen count can reach high levels from April to October.

Winter days can be delightful; bitingly cold temperatures are compensated for by bright blue skies. Sudden snowfalls send New Yorkers to Central Park, for sledding and skiing, particularly on Pilgrim Hill on the East Side. True blizzards, however, are not common in the city.

Summer temperatures often soar above 90°F (32°C) and higher, with very high humidity especially during July and August.

Enjoy a memorable horse-drawn carriage ride through lively Central Park on a sunny Sunday afternoon – in summer or winter!

CALENDAR OF EVENTS

Any excuse goes for a parade or celebration in New York, where residents have a knack for presenting a grand spectacle. Fifth Avenue is *en fête* several times a year, and free concerts and Shakespeare plays are performed in the summer *(see p 62)*.

January/February

Late January **Chinese New Year:** the actual date varies, but it is celebrated on the first full moon after January 19, with a parade and fireworks in Chinatown. Early February **Empire State Building Run-Up**: a dash to the 86th floor (no, not on the outside) for those intent on proving their physical fitness.

All February **Black History Month**: African-American heritage is celebrated in different parts of the city.

March/April

March 17 **St. Patrick's Day Parade**: Fifth Avenue gets a green stripe painted along its length for this huge Irish festival, which draws in the whole city – Irish or not – in its enthusiasm. The parade starts at Fifth Avenue and 44th Street at 11am.

Late March/April **Easter Parade**: New Yorkers stroll about to display their spring finery on Easter Sunday on Fifth Avenue from 49th to 57th streets.

May/June

Mid May **Martin Luther King Jr. Parade**: The civil rights leader is remembered in a Fifth Avenue march from 61st to 79th Streets. Late May (Sunday) **AIDS Walk New York**: About 40,000 people follow a 6.2 mi route from Central Park's Sheep Meadow to raise funds for people living with HIV or AIDS. May/June **Washington Square Outdoor Art Exhibit**: A free five-day Greenwich Village fair with works by some 300 artists on sale. Early June **National Puerto Rican Day Parade**: Fifth Avenue teems with marching bands and floats. Late June **Lesbian and Gay Pride Week Celebrations**: The week ends with a parade on Fifth Avenue, from 52nd Street to Christopher Street.

July/August

July **Independence Day**: Macy's sponsors a big fireworks show over the East River. Celebrations are held in all the boroughs. July/August **Free New York Philharmonic concerts**: In

Central Park and other major parks.

July/August **Shakespeare in the Park**: Tickets for the Central Park shows are free, on a first-come, first-served basis, but getting a ticket may mean arriving early and waiting most of the day. (A large tree-ringed area immediately outside the theater entrance is an ideal place to pass the time.)

Early-mid August **Harlem Week**: Multi-activity African-American and Hispanic festival.

September/October

1st Monday in September **West Indian Carnival Parade**: In Brooklyn, with Caribbean-style music on Eastern Parkway from Utica Avenue to Grand Army Plaza.

Mid-September **Feast of San Gennaro**: 11 days of celebrations in Little Italy.

September/October **New York Film Festival**: Lasts three weeks at Lincoln Center.

2nd Monday in October **Columbus Day Parade**: On Fifth Avenue.

31 October **Halloween Parade**: In Greenwich Village, along Sixth Avenue from Spring Street to 22nd Street.

November/December

1st Sunday in November **New York City Marathon**: Starts with 30,000 runners on Staten Island and ends at the Tavern on the Green restaurant in Central Park (West Side).

4th Thursday in November **Macy's Thanksgiving Day Parade**: Central Park West to Herald Square.

Early December **Lighting of the Giant Christmas Tree**: At Rockefeller Center.

December 31st **New Year's Eve Countdown**: At Times Square.

ACCOMMODATIONS

New York offers a wide range of accommodations that includes hotels of all classes, bed-and-breakfast inns or suites in private homes, apartment hotels with fully furnished suites and maid service, and budget hotels and hostels.

Prices range from $375 or more per night (double room) at elegant hotels on Fifth, Park and Madison avenues, to lower priced hotels ($125-295/night) in the theater district, and budget hotels ($90-145/night) scattered throughout Manhattan.

For information on all aspects of staying in New York, consult the *Official NYC Guide*, available free from the Times Square Visitors Center, 46th and Broadway, or from the city tourist bureau's Official Visitor

Independence Day celebrations explode with sights and sounds.

Information Center, 810 Seventh Avenue, between 52nd and 53rd streets.

Accommodations in the city are very much in demand, so make reservations well in

advance of your visit–
particularly in summer or over
holidays.

Hotels/Motels
Many hotels offer packages
including lodging, breakfast,
sightseeing tours, restaurant or
theater bookings at significant
savings.
Major hotel chains in New York
include:

Best Western	☎ 800/528-1234
Comfort Inn	☎ 800/228-5150
Hilton	☎ 800/445-8667
Holiday Inn	☎ 800/465-4329
Hyatt	☎ 800/233-1234
Marriott	☎ 800/228-9290
Sheraton	☎ 800/325-3535
Westin	☎ 800/228-3000

Hotel Reservation Services
Accommodations Express
☎ 800/444-7666

Central Reservation Service
☎ 800/548-3311
Concordia Hotel Reservations
☎ 800/730-4778
Express Hotel Reservations
☎ 800/356-1123
CityRes ☎ 800/468-3593

Bed & Breakfast/Apartments
Many B&Bs are privately owned
historic homes ($75-150/night)
or apartments, and often
include continental breakfast.
Private baths are not always
available. A minimum stay of
two nights is often required.

B&B Reservation Services
The Cheapest Bed and
Breakfast ☎ 212/307-9177
City Lights Bed & Breakfast
☎ 212/737-7049
Gamut Realty Group
☎ 800/437-8353
New World B&B
☎ 800/443-3800

*Relish the
spectacular lighting
displays and
holiday decorations
at renowned
Rockefeller Center,
with its towering
Christmas tree and
ice rink filled with
skaters.*

Zabar's Deli, Upper West Side.

Hostels/Budget Accommodations
Hostels and budget accommodations in New York offer basic dormitory sleeping or a private room for a higher rate ($25-$75/night).

YMCA Guest Rooms
224 E. 47th St. (Midtown)
☎ 212/756-9600; 5 W. 63rd St.
(Uptown) ☎ 212/875-4273

A selection of hostels:
Chelsea International Youth Hostel, 251 W. 20th St.

☎ 212/647-0010
Gershwin Hotel 7 E. 27th St.
☎ 212/545-8000
Chelsea Center 313 W. 29th St.
☎ 212/643-0214
Big Apple Hostel 119 W. 45th St.
☎ 212/302-2603
Banana Bungalow Jazz on the Park Hostel
36th W. 106th St.
☎ 800-6HOSTEL
Hostelling International
891 Amsterdam Ave.
☎ 212/932-2300.

The Hard Rock Cafe – a perfect place for music lovers to eat and drink.

FOOD AND DRINK

New York City is famous for the number of its restaurants – over 18,000 – and the sheer range of cuisine. New Yorkers are demanding, and any restaurant must work hard to establish and maintain its reputation. The average cost of a meal is $37.

Many New Yorkers eat out several times a week, and they choose a restaurant not only for the quality of the food, but for the creative genius of the chef, the grandeur of the decor, and the efficiency and professionalism of the serving staff. The simplest establishments – coffee shops, delis, steakhouses and noodle shops – offer a relaxed atmosphere, with quick, friendly service.

In true New York fashion, you

might combine an enjoyable meal with the sport of people-watching. Many New York restaurants, bars and coffee-houses have glassed-in sidewalk extensions, and outdoor cafés flourish during the summer. This happens all over the city, in modest little places and at lively, ever-popular ones like Nadine's in Greenwich Village, where Michelle Pfeiffer, Martina Navratilova and Robert de Niro have been known to hang out.

De Niro is a co-owner of the movie memorabilia palace **Planet Hollywood**, at 45th Street and Broadway in Times Square, where you can find a wide choice of traditional American food at a reasonable price.

Themed restaurants like the **Hard Rock Cafe**, 221 W. 57th Street, put the emphasis on noise rather than food, but that's all part of the atmosphere.

If you want to try the cuisine of distant lands, New York is the place to do it. You can find all the popular world cuisines here, with a vast choice of less well-known culinary offerings from Afghan and Burmese, to Tibetan and Vietnamese. Chinese food isn't confined to Chinatown, though that is a must-try area. And you can sate yourself with hearty soups at **Mee Noodle**

Shops on First, Second and Ninth avenues. Italian meals are offered in nearly 350 eateries throughout all the boroughs, at both ends of the price range.

The Theater District (west Forties) offers more than 250 options for pre-show, post-show and during-the-show customers. At many of the eateries in the district you will come across Broadway actors taking a break between peformances or rehearsals.

Places to Eat

A unique dining experience can be found on almost any block of New York City. Below is a sample of some of the city's more popular and well-frequented establishments. The type of cuisine and an indication of price is given:
$ = inexpensive
$$ = moderate
$$$ = expensive
Reservations are recommended for $$ and $$$ restaurants.

Lower Manhattan
Fraunces Tavern Restaurant 54 Pearl St. ☎ 212/968-1776 (American $$$).
Harbour Lights Pier 17, 3rd Floor ☎ 212/227-2800 (Seafood $$$).
Bridge Café 279 Water St. ☎ 212/227-3344 (American $$$).

A New York street vendor selling pretzels.

Chinatown – Litte Italy
Silver Palace 50 Bowery
☎ 212/964-1204 (Dim Sum
$$).
Peking Duck House 28 Mott St.
☎ 212/227-1810 (Chinese $$).
Nice Restaurant 35 E. Broadway
☎ 212/406-9510 (Cantonese $$).
Triple 8 Palace Restaurant
88 E. Broadway (top floor)
☎ 212/941-8886 (Chinese $$).
La Mela 167 Mulberry St.
☎ 212/431-9493 (Neapolitan $).
Puglia 189 Hester St. ☎ 212/
966-6006 (Southern Italian $).

SoHo – Tribeca
Nobu 105 Hudson St.
☎ 212/219-0500 (Japanese $$$).
Tribeca Grill 375 Greenwich St.
☎ 212/941-3900 (American $$$).
The Odeon 145 W. Broadway
☎ 212/233-0507 (Continental
$$).
Zoë 90 Prince St. ☎ 212/966-
6722 (American $$$).

Greenwich Village – Chelsea
Gotham Bar & Grill 12 E. 12th
St. ☎ 212/620-4020 (American
$$$).
Cornelia Street Café 29
Cornelia St. ☎ 212/989-9319
(New American $$).

Home 20 Cornelia St. ☎ 212/243-9579 (American $$).
El Cid 322 W. 15th St. ☎ 212/929-9332 (Spanish $).

East Village
2nd Avenue Deli 156 Second Ave. ☎ 212/677-0606 (Jewish $$).
First 87 First Ave. ☎ 212/674-3823 (Eclectic $$).
Boca Chica 13 First Ave. ☎ 212/473-0108 (South American $).

Midtown
Oyster Bar and Restaurant Grand Central Teminal ☎ 212/490-6650 (Seafood $$$).
The Four Seasons 99 E. 52nd St. ☎ 212/754-9494 (Continental $$$).
Rosa Mexicano 1063 First Ave. ☎ 212/753-7407 (Mexican $$).

Upper East Side
E.A.T. 1064 Madison Ave. ☎ 212/772-0022 (American $$$).
Sarabeth's Kitchen 1295 Madison Ave. ☎ 212/410-7335 (American $$).

Midtown market.

Upper West Side and Harlem
Tavern on the Green Central Park West at 67th St. ☎ 212/873-3200 (American $$$).
Sylvia's 328 Lenox Ave. ☎ 212/996-0660 (Southern $$).
The Cotton Club 656 W. 125th St. ☎ 212/663-7980 (Southern $$).

Tavern On The Green, in Central Park West, is a New York Institution.

Fast Food

The main requirements for a quick snack are that it is tasty and reasonably priced. You can sometimes eat it where you buy it, or you may want to take it back to your hotel or sit out in Central Park or on the steps of the Library on Fifth Avenue. New Yorkers have turned fast food into an art form.

Under this general heading comes an amazing variety of foods. The most widespread is the **pizza parlor**, where you can get a single slice or a whole pie, with every imaginable topping, to take home and eat. Many pizza places claim to be "the original" or simply "the best," and each has its devotees who will often travel some distance just for a slice.

There are a number of **hamburger restaurants**, where the burger of your choice will be served with French fries, a selection of toppings and a drink, all within a few minutes. **Bagel shops** have sprung up all over the city. You pick the kind you want (with poppy or sesame seeds, or garlic or onion) and eat it plain or make it a

Carnegie Deli, on Seventh Avenue, is a New York legend.

sandwich – cream cheese, smoked salmon, turkey and more!).

Delicatessens should not be overlooked in your search. The variety of foods they serve is often dictated by the nationality of the owner. Almost all have good quality cold meats and cheeses, and all make up sandwiches and tubs of salads. Italian delis have pastas to die for, and a kosher deli will have special meats, kosher pickles and, of course, New York-style cheesecake for dessert.

Hot pretzels are sold from stalls on street corners throughout the city, and provide welcome refreshment for visitors on the move. Finally, you can't talk about New York fast food and not mention the **hot dog**. These have been sold from street carts and at delis for decades.

And so to Drink…

Coffeehouses serve tasty food quickly, but also give you the chance to sit and enjoy it at your leisure. The typical coffeehouse specializes in coffee drinks including cappuccinos, lattés, and a host of pastries for breakfast. Many establishments also offer a

Macy's Christmas decorations are spectacular every year.

selection of soups, sandwiches and salads for lunch.

A selection of Greenwich Village coffeehouses:
Café Borgia (185 Bleecker St.) An atmospheric old-world coffeehouse with a buzzing late-night clientele.
Caffè Sha Sha (510 Hudson St.) Sample the fine coffee, ice cream and pastries in summer on the pleasant back patio.
Tea and Sympathy (108 Greenwich Ave.) Very cozy, very British spot for afternoon tea and scones.
Caffè Reggio (119 MacDougal St.) New York's oldest café, with outdoor tables in summer.
Caffè Vivaldi (32 Jones St.) A real fireplace and authentic fin-de-siècle Vienna coffeehouse atmosphere.
Caffè Rafaella (134 Seventh Ave. South) Charming, whacky café, with delicious pastries.

There are hundreds of **bars, pubs and taverns** throughout the city, many frequented as much for their unpretentious food as for their libations. Tops on the tourist trail are **McSorley's Old Ale House** (15 E. 7th St.), an East Village Irish saloon dating from 1854, and the **White Horse Tavern** (567 Hudson St.), where Welsh poet Dylan Thomas had the last drink of his life.

A growing and popular phenomenon is the **microbrewery**, offering a variety of beers brewed on the premises.

SHOPPING

You can shop your way across Manhattan, the borough with the widest choice. The key is to know what you want and where you want to go. Most stores open at 10am and close at 6pm, though some stay open later on Thursday or Friday. On Sundays opening hours are usually from noon until 6pm. So plan your route, eat a good breakfast and shop 'til you drop.

Fifth Avenue

Most visitors who regard shopping as a priority make a beeline for Fifth Avenue. Most of the city's department stores are here, between 34th and 60th streets, including **Lord & Taylor** (424 Fifth Ave.), **Saks Fifth Avenue** (611 Fifth Ave.), **Takashimaya** (693 Fifth Ave.), **Henri Bendel** (712 Fifth Ave.) and **Bergdorf Goodman** (754 Fifth Ave.). Scattered among the retail giants are specialty shops, toy stores and designer boutiques such as **Tiffany**, **Cartier**, **Gucci**, **Elizabeth Arden** and **Fortunoff**.

For a study in vintage '80s decadence, browse through the boutiques of **Trump Tower** (between 56th and 57th Streets), embellished with waterfalls and Italian marble.

Oshkosh B'Gosh, at 47th Street, offers bright, practical clothes in sturdy fabrics that are a hit with parents and children alike. The company originally made overalls for farmers and railroadmen.

Upper East Side

East of Fifth Avenue and Uptown, **Madison Avenue** between 72nd and 59th Streets features specialty shops and designer boutiques. At **Ralph Lauren** (867 Madison Ave.) the Polo look is alive and kicking. Try the ready to wear sections in **Emanuel Ungaro** (792 Madison Ave.), **Valentino** (747 Madison Ave.) or **Giorgio Armani** (760 Madison Ave.). Farther south is the Uptown branch of **Barneys** (600 Madison Ave.), a nine-story fashion emporium, while the latest **Calvin Klein** store (654 Madison Ave.) offers furniture alongside the famous jeans.

Bloomingdale's, on Lexington Avenue, between 59th and 60th streets, is famous throughout the world and sells a wide range of goods, including clothing. Imported clothes by Valentino and other designers fill boutiques within the store.

Lower West Side and Flatiron
Anchoring the Lower West Side shipping corridors of Broadway and Sixth and Fifth avenues is **Macy's** – "the world's largest department store" – on Broadway at 34th Street. You can find almost everything for sale here in the store's small individual shops.

Just south of Macy's, in the Manhattan Mall at 33rd Street and Sixth Avenue, is **Electronics Boutique,** renowned for its

Bloomingdale's is an unforgettable New York experience.

computer products and knowledgeable sales staff. **Sephora** and **H&M** have recently opened Herald Square locations.

Between 14th and 23rd superstores such as **Bed, Bath and Beyond** (620 Sixth Ave.) have taken their place next to old favorites. Clothier **Barney's,** has returned to the neighborhood of its birth with the opening of its lower-cost Barney's Co-op (236 W. 18th St.). **Weiss and Mahoney** (142 Fifth Ave.) has been selling army-navy surplus for

generations. The flagship **Barnes and Noble** bookstore (105 Fifth Ave.) is a block south. And nearby are behemoths **ABC Carpet and Home** (Broadway and 19th St.) and **Paragon Sports** (Broadway and 18th St.).

Brand-name fashions and furs can be found in the **Garment District** of Seventh Avenue (30th-40th Sts.), north of Chelsea. Look for notices of sales open to the public in manufacturers' showrooms.

Beyond Fashion

Winding streets lined with small shops selling antiques, toys and offbeat clothes lend **Greenwich Village** a special charm. **SoHo**, once a region of dilapidated warehouses, has been transformed into a popular arts and high-fashion shopping spot.

Bookworms will find New York a paradise. "Wise men fish here" is the motto at **Gotham Book Mart** (41 W 47th St.), one of many smaller specialty, new and secondhand book stores.

CompUSA on 57th Street and Broadway stocks more than 5,000 computer-related goods.

An unusual and interesting gift shop, the **New York Exchange for Woman's Work** provides an outlet for needy women who make toys,

children's clothes, various craft items and foods. The Exchange is located at 149 E. 60th Street between Lexington and Third avenues.

UNICEF gift and card shops raise funds to help the under-privileged children in the world. UNICEF can be found at 3 United Nations Plaza on 44th Street, and it also has shops in the UN Building at the UN Counter, and at the NYU Bookstore at 18 Washington Place, as well as Bloomingdale's and Pier 1 Imports stores.

Photography buffs should not miss **B & H Photo** (420 9th Ave. between 33rd and 34th St.), a store full of cameras and all the equipment and gadgetry that goes with them. Prices are good and the multilingual staff helpful.

Although primarily a place where professional musicians buy their instruments, **Manny's Music**, founded more than 65 years ago at 156 W. 48th Street at Seventh Avenue, is a magnet for rock-and-roll fans. On the walls, hang 3,000 photographs of famous customers, including The Beatles and Jimi Hendrix, and there's always the chance of coming face to face with world-renowned groups like U2.

Carnegie Hall is New York's most famous concert venue.

ENTERTAINMENT AND NIGHTLIFE

The entertainment capital of the world, New York offers a 24-hour kaleidoscope of dance, concerts, opera, jazz, rock, musicals, film and theater, clubs and cabarets.

The best sources for entertainment information are the *New York Times* (especially the Sunday Arts & Leisure and the Friday Weekend sections), and *New York Magazine*, the *New Yorker*, *Time Out New York* and the *Village Voice*. Listings and the official **Broadway Theater Guide** are available free from NYC & Company, the city's visitor bureau.

Ballet and Dance

Balletomanes and modern dance aficionados will certainly feel at home in New York, where there are around a dozen top-class companies that present performances year-round.

The **American Ballet Theatre** performs a repertoire of traditional classics and contemporary works from May to July at the Metropolitan Opera House and at Lincoln Center (☎ 212/362-6000). The New York State Theater (☎ 212/496-0600), also at the Lincoln Center, is home to the **New York City Ballet**, a company of 90 dancers. Its seasons there run from November to February and April to June.

City Center Theatre, 131 W. 55th Street between 6th and 7th avenues (☎ 212/581-7907), serves as a venue for renowned local companies such as the Alvin Ailey Dance Company, the Paul Taylor Dance Company, and as home to American Ballet Theatre's fall season. The Joyce Theater, at 175 8th Avenue and 19th Street in Chelsea (☎ 212/242-0800) has been presenting contemporary dance since 1982. In addition, younger members of the Merce Cunningham Company offer modern works at the Merce Cunningham Studio on the 11th floor at Westbeth, 55 Bethune Street.

Concerts and Opera

The city's best-known musical venues are **Carnegie Hall** (57th St. and Seventh Ave. ☎ 212/247-7800) and Lincoln Center's **Avery Fisher Hall**, (☎ 212/875-5030); the **Metropolitan Opera House**, (☎ 212/362-6000); and **New York State Theater** (☎ 212/870-5570). Aside from these, there are many other lesser known places where you can hear good music.

The Amato Opera Theater, 319 Bowery, stages performances by young, talented musicians and singers. Chamber music is performed aboard **Bargemusic**, moored in the shadow of the Brooklyn Bridge off Fulton Ferry Landing, Brooklyn Heights. The eminent Brooklyn Academy of Music, better known as **BAM**, occasionally works with the Metropolitan Opera on innovative opera productions and new works. The **Grace Rainey Rogers Auditorium** at the Metropolitan Museum of Art, presents performances of classical music by well-known artists.

Film and Theater

It has been said that there is a choice of almost 200 films on any night in New York. They include the latest Hollywood blockbusters and foreign-language films. Consult newspapers and periodicals

The world-famous Rockettes perform at Radio City Music Hall.

such as *Time Out New York, The New Yorker* and *New York Magazine.* You can usually reserve tickets by dialing ☎ 212/777-FILM – have your credit card handy.

More professional theater is produced in New York than in the rest of the United States, and one of the city's enduring images is one of flashing neon lights proclaiming shows and stars along the Great White Way – as Broadway is dubbed. The Broadway of old consisted of 50-odd theaters clustered around Times Square. Today, the city's **Theater District** stretches between Broadway and Seventh Avenue and 40th and 53rd Streets.

Off Broadway theaters seat fewer than 500; most are located in or around the Theater District or downtown. They offer more challenging productions than

Map showing some of the major Broadway theaters.

their Broadway brethren. **Off-Off Broadway** theaters with fewer than 100 seats may be further out, both geographically and artistically.

Theater-going in New York is expensive, but the cost can be reduced by buying half-price tickets on the day of the performance at TKTS booths in Times Square and the South Street Seaport at John and Front streets.

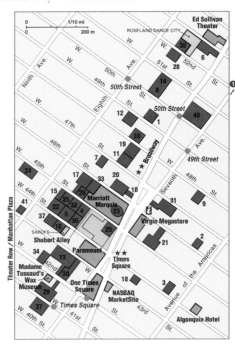

ENTERTAINMENT AND NIGHTLIFE

1 **Ambassador Theater**
   (219 W. 49th St. ☎ 239-6200)
2 **American Place Theater**
   (111 W. 46th St. ☎ 239-6200)
3 **Belasco Theater**
   (111 W. 44th St. ☎ 239-6200)
4 **Booth Theater**
   (222 W. 45th St. ☎ 239-6200)
5 **Broadhurst Theater**
   (235 W. 44th St. ☎ 239-6200)
6 **Broadway Theater**
   (1681 Broadway, ☎ 239-6200)
7 **Brooks Atkinson Theater**
   (256 W. 47th St. ☎ 307-4100)
8 **Circle in the Square**
   (1633 Broadway, ☎ 307-2704)
9 **Cort Theater**
   (138 W. 48th St. ☎ 239-6200)
10 **Duffy Theatre**
   (1553 Broadway, ☎ 921-7862)
11 **Ethel Barrymore Theater**
   (243 W. 47TH ST. ☎ 239-6200)
12 **Eugene O'Neill Theater**
   (230 W. 49th St. ☎ 239-6200)
13 **Ford Center for Performing Arts**
   (213 W. 42nd St. ☎ 556-4750)
14 **Gershwin Theater**
   (222 W. 51st St. ☎ 586-6510)
15 **John Golden Theater**
   (252 W. 45th St. ☎ 239-6200)
16 **Helen Hayes Theater**
   (240 W. 44th St. ☎ 944-9450)
17 **Imperial Theater**
   (249 W. 45th St. ☎ 239-6200)
18 **Lambs Theater**
   (140 W. 44th St. ☎ 997-1780)
19 **Longacre Theater**
   (220 W. 48th St. ☎ 239-6200)
20 **Lunt-Fontanne Theater**
   (205 W. 46th St. ☎ 575-9200)
21 **Lyceum Theater**
   (149 W. 45th St. ☎ 239-6200)
22 **Majestic Theater**
   (247 W. 44th St. ☎ 239-6200)
23 **Marquis Theater**
   (1535 Broadway, ☎ 382-0100)

24 **Martin Beck Theater**
   (302 W. 45th St. ☎ 239-6200)
25 **Minskoff Theater**
   (200 W. 45th St. ☎ 869-0550)
26 **Music Box Theater**
   (239 W. 45th St. ☎ 239-6200)
27 **Nederlander Theater**
   (208 W. 41st St. ☎ 921-8000)
28 **Neil Simon Theater**
   (250 W. 52nd St. ☎ 757-8646)
29 **New AmsterdamTheater**
   (214 W. 42nd St. ☎ 282-2900)
30 **New Victory Theater**
   (207-211 W. 42nd St. ☎ 564-4222)
31 **Palace Theater**
   (1564 Broadway, ☎ 730-8200)
32 **Plymouth Theater**
   (236 W. 45th St. ☎ 239-6200)
33 **Richard Rodgers Theater**
   (226 W. 46th St. ☎ 221-1211)
35 **Royale Theater**
   (242 W. 45th St. ☎ 239-6200)
36 **Shubert Theater**
   (225 W. 44th St. ☎ 239-6200)
37 **St. James' Theater**
   (246 W. 44th St. ☎ 239-6200)
38 **Virginia Theater**
   (245 W. 52nd St. ☎ 239-6200)
39 **Walter Kerr Theater**
   (219 W. 48th St. ☎ 239-6200)
40 **Winter Garden Theater**
   (1634 Broadway, ☎ 239-6200)

Theaters not shown on the map:
• **Actors Studio**
  (432 W. 44th St. ☎ 757-0870)
• **Blue Angel Theater**
  (323 W. 44th St. ☎ 262-3333)
• **Douglas Fairbanks Theater**
  (432 W. 42nd St. ☎ 239-4321)
• **New Dramatists**
  (424 W. 44th St. ☎ 757-6960)
• **Westside Theater**
  (407 W. 43rd St. ☎ 315-2244)

Clubs and Discos

This is the alternative New York – a whole subculture of dancing and live music covering the entire spectrum of popular sound. A few places have a jacket-and-tie dress code, but most allow more casual clothing.

Warehouse-size dance clubs such as **Sound Factory** (618 W. 46th St.) pound thousands of ravers with tens of thousands of watts of amp power. Smaller clubs abound as well; they can slide from hot to old news to extinction in a New York minute. It's best to check listings in the *Village Voice* or *Time Out New York* before raging into the night.

Cabaret

New York cabaret covers all styles, from the more upscale Uptown style to the refreshingly unsophisticated ambience of Downtown locations.

The Oak Room at the Algonquin Hotel, 59 W. 44th Street (☎ 212/840-6800), was frequented by New York's literati in the days of Dorothy Parker, James Thurber and their Round Table companions. Cabaret continues here as if the last 50 years hadn't happened.

The Cotton Club, another famous name, is back in business. Originally located on Lenox Avenue in Harlem, the club launched the likes of Cab Calloway, Duke Ellington and Lena Horne. Now the show goes on at 666 W. 125th Street.

At the **Cafe Carlyle,** 35 E. 76th Street (☎ 212/744-1600), Bobby Short has been playing the most sophisticated of standards for three decades.

Downtown, there are dozens of cabarets (the publications named on p.97 will tell you

Times Square ente

who's doing what and where).

Jazz

A trip to New York would not be complete without an evening of jazz. All but the last three of those listed below are in Greenwich Village; the others are worth a trip north.

Blue Note Jazz Club (131 W. 3rd St. ☎ 212/475-8592) Incredible acoustics and a stellar lineup make this the city's premier jazz club.

Bottom Line Cabaret (15 E. 4th St. ☎ 212/228-6300) Also good for rock and folk music.

Smalls (183 W. 10th St. ☎ 212/929-7565) A snug, cave setting and funky Village crowd; sessions go on until morning.

Tonk (107 Norfolk St. ☎ 212/358-7501) The new Lower East Side hot spot for

nent.

avant-garde jazz.

Village Vanguard (178 Seventh Ave. South ☎ 212/255-4037) New York's oldest jazz club.

Cajun (129 Eighth Ave. at W. 16th St. ☎ 212/691-6174) A Manhattan slice of New Orleans with Dixieland jazz.

Iridium (1650 Broadway at 51st St. ☎ 212/582-2121) Serious jazz in the most playful setting imaginable.

Birdland (315 W. 44th St. ☎ 212/581-3080) Classy ultra-cool Midtown venue; Southern cuisine.

SPORTS

There are lots of places where you can catch a game, ranging from Madison Square Garden in Midtown, to the USTA National Tennis Center at Flushing Meadows-Corona Park in Queens and the Meadowlands Sports Complex in East Rutherford, New Jersey. **Tickets** can generally be purchased at the venue or through **Ticketmaster** ☎ 212/307-7171.

Madison Square Garden is the city's most central sports venue, located above Penn Station between 31st and 33rd streets at Seventh Avenue. It seats more than 20,000 spectators and stages a variety of sporting events throughout the year. Visitors might have difficulty obtaining tickets for major sporting events. Contact the box office for information ☎ 212/465-6741. If you don't make it to the big game, race or fight, check out the big screen in one of New York's numerous sports bars.

Football

New York's major football teams are the Jets (☎ 516/560-8200) and the Giants (☎ 201/935-8111), and although the loyalty each receives splits the city down the middle, both play at the **Giants Stadium** in East Rutherford, New Jersey. The football season is from September to the end of December. The Super Bowl takes place on the fourth Sunday in January.

Baseball

The baseball season lasts from April to October, and games involving the New York Yankees and the New York Mets are a major talking point in bars and taxis. The Yankees play at **Yankee Stadium** in the Bronx (☎ 718/293-6000), and the Mets' home ground is **Shea Stadium** in Queens (☎ 718/507-8499). The climax of the baseball season comes in October when the champion teams of the National League and the American League meet

in the World Series.

Basketball

Fast and graceful, basketball is played from October to April. The city's major teams are the Knickerbockers – known as the Knicks – and the New Jersey Nets. The Knicks play at **Madison Square Garden** and the Nets at the **Continental Airlines Arena** in East Rutherford, New Jersey.

Horse Racing

Both thoroughbred and harness race meets are held at the **Meadowlands** (☎ 201/ 843-2446) Trotting races take place between January and August and flat racing from September to November.

Evening harness races are staged throughout the year at **Yonkers Raceway** (☎ 914/968-4200), in Westchester County just north of New York City.

The **Aqueduct** (☎ 718/641-4700), in Ozone Park, Queens, is known as 'The Big A' to fans, while **Belmont Park** (☎ 516/488-6000), just across the city line on Long Island, is home to the Belmont Stakes, one of the three big races of the US Triple Crown.

Ice Hockey

Fast and furious, ice hockey is played from October to April, and New Yorkers follow the activities of three major teams. The NY Islanders play their home games at **Nassau Memorial Coliseum**, in Uniondale, Long Island. The NY Rangers are based at **Madison Square Garden**, while the NJ Devils' home rink is at the **Continental Airlines Arena** in East Rutherford, New Jersey.

Tennis

You need two things to get decent tickets for the semi-finals and finals of the **US Open** Tennis Championships held at the **USTA National Tennis Center** at Flushing Meadows-Corona Park: time and money. A limited number of bleacher seats – bare wooden planks under an open sky – in the Arthur Ashe Stadium are available on a first-come, first-served basis. The Open takes place in September. Day passes for earlier rounds, however, are easier to obtain. For information ☎ 718/760-6200.

THE BASICS

Note: This guide is intended for both US and overseas visitors. Some details therefore will not apply to everyone. Sections of particular reference to non-US residents are marked with an asterisk [*].

Before You Go *

Citizens of countries participating in the Visa Waiver Program planning on staying in the US as ordinary tourists for a period of up to 90 days do not need a visitor's visa. All that is required is a valid passport, and a visa waiver form, which may be obtained in advance from a travel agent, or provided by the airline during check-in. This form must be handed in to immigration on arrival. Certain categories of visitor, such as those planning to do business within the US, need a visa.

Visitors from countries outside the program require a valid passport and a non-immigrant visitor's visa. Details are available from the nearest US embassy or consulate. Vaccinations are not required.

Getting There *

Most transatlantic flights land at **John F. Kennedy International Airport** (JFK) (☎ 718/244-4444), while **LaGuardia Airport** (LGA)

(☎ 718/533-3400) receives mostly domestic flights. Both airports are in Queens, a one and a quarter hours and a 45min drive respectively from Manhattan, depending on the traffic. International and domestic flights fly into **Newark Liberty International Airport** in New Jersey, about a 1hr drive from Manhattan.

There are countless ticket prices and travel deals to New York, and you should shop around. Low-cost flights can often be arranged through travel agents who specialize in long-distance flights, or by booking a charter flight. APEX or Super-APEX tickets may be purchased directly from the airlines.

Fly-drive and flight-plus-accommodation offers are often less expensive than booking everything separately. Brochures on these types of vacations are available from travel agents.

Arriving *

If you are a non-US citizen coming from outside the country, you must complete immigration and customs declaration forms during the flight, and hand them in once you land. You will be asked where you plan to spend the first night, and when you intend to leave the country. You might also be asked to prove that you can support yourself financially during your stay, and any indication that you cannot might result in admission being refused.

To expedite your progress through customs, pay special attention to Question 9 on your declaration form; this relates to fruit, plants, meats, food, soil, live animals (including birds) and farm products.

Transportation from the Airport

The easiest and cheapest way of getting from all three airports is by bus. **New York Airport Service** express buses run between JFK and LaGuardia Airports and Grand Central Terminal and Port Authority Bus Terminal. **Super Shuttle** offers shared mini-bus rides to and from the airports. **Olympia**

Airport Express Bus Service. runs a service from Newark Airport to Manhattan every 20mins (4am-11:45pm).

Taxis are available outside each terminal. Passengers should wait in line and allow a dispatcher to hail the next available cab for them. Fares to Manhattan: from JFK, $35 flat rate plus tolls; from LGA, $16 to $26 plus tolls (metered fare dependent on distance and traffic); from Newark, $40 to $60, plus tolls. Remember to add a tip to any taxi fare *(see p 123)* More costly private car services are also available.

Trains from other parts of the country arrive at either Grand Central Terminal (42nd St. and Park Ave.) or Penn Station (Seventh Ave. and 33rd St.) The Port Authority Bus Terminal (42nd St. and Eighth Ave.), is the arrival point for most bus lines, including Greyhound.

Surveying the city from the Met's rooftop garden.

A-Z

Accidents and Breakdowns

Cars rented in New York State have a collision damage waiver (CDW) included in the price by law. Generally renters can not be held liable for more than a $100 deductible if the car is damaged or stolen. If you are renting outside of New York State, purchasing a CDW may be worthwhile.

An emergency telephone number will be given to you in case your rental car breaks down. A mobile phone can be rented from the car agency, and will offer a lifeline in an emergency. If you do have car problems, call 911 on your mobile phone or get the car to the side of the road, lift the front hood and wait for the highway patrol or state police to come by. Women driving alone should not advertise the fact that they are in trouble.

Accommodations *see p 82*

Airports *see p 108*

Babysitters *see p 112*

Banks

Banks are open Monday to Thursday, 9am-3pm; Friday 9am-5pm, although longer opening hours are becoming more normal. Some banks open on Saturdays. Most banks change foreign travelers' checks and currency, though it may be cheaper to conduct these transactions at exchange services, since they charge a lower commission.

Visitors from around the world have access to cash withdrawals, using major credit cards and bank cards at automated teller machines available at most banks. Get lists of outlets and charges from your home bank before you leave.

Beaches

There are fine beaches on Long Island relatively close to Manhattan. Closer to the city, Coney Island in Brooklyn and Orchard Beach in the Bronx and Rockaway Beach in Queens offer a sandy refuge from the city *(see p 74)*.

Bicycles

Outlets that offer bikes for rent, such as the **Loeb Memorial Boathouse** (☎ 212/517-2233) in Central Park, can be found in the Yellow Pages. The latter is particularly convenient if you

The Plaza Hotel, with a statue of General Sherman in the foreground.

plan to follow the several miles of bicycle paths within the park.

Buses *see p 125*

Car Rental*

Cars are widely available through airports, hotels or individual rental companies. The minimum rental age is 21, although some companies impose an age limit of 25, and others increase insurance premiums for those under 25. You will be expected to pay by credit card, and if you don't have one, a large deposit may be required.

Most of the major car-rental firms have offices in Manhattan, the outer boroughs and at the three city airports. The average daily rates for a compact car, with unlimited mileage for 5-7 days, ranges from $40-60. Note that rental cars are taxed 13.25% (not included in the advertised rates).

Avis	☎ 800/331-1212
Budget	☎ 800/527-0700
Dollar	☎ 800/421-6868
Enterprise	☎ 800/325-8007
Hertz	☎ 800/654-3131
National	☎ 800/227-7368

Arranging a fly/drive package or booking a car before arriving in New York can be extremely economical. Try to get free unlimited mileage, and note that there will probably be a drop-off charge for leaving the car somewhere other than where you rented it. If you are renting a car outside New York State, check your rental agreement for mention of collision damage waiver (CDW) – if this is not included in the price, seriously consider adding it *(see p 110)*.

Children

Many hotels allow children to stay in their parents' room free of charge, while others offer special children's rates. Inquire about any children's activities that the hotel might offer, or ask if there is a babysitting service.

New York is packed with interesting things for children to do and see, including two special museums for children, zoos, parks, nearby beaches, and many special events organized by theaters and libraries for children during the summer months.

Events for children are listed in the Weekend section of the Friday *New York Times*, in *Time Out New York* and on the flier *New York for Kids*, which is available from the Times Square Visitor Center, between 46th and 47th and Broadway *(see also p 72)*.

A few hints on where to eat

Mickey Mantle's
Check out the sports memorabillia museum, watch games on the numerous televisions and enjoy a plate of hickory-smoked ribs at this restaurant named after a famous New York Yankee.

Mars 2112
Take a ride on a UFO to the unknown world of Mars where you will find food, games and even aliens!

Churches *see p 122*

Climate *see p 80*

Clothing*
Informality is the keynote in the US, and comfortable clothing is essential for the busy tourist. Some restaurants are very formal and it is wise to check before you reserve a table. Similarly, smart dress should be worn for the ballet, opera and most theaters.

Remember that evenings can be considerably cooler than the daytime, and air-conditioning makes theaters, restaurants and stores quite chilly, so an extra sweater or jacket can be essential.

A visitor from the UK will find that women's clothing sizes are always a size less. Men's suits and shirts are identical to UK sizes. Shoe sizes are 1 to 1.5 above British ones. A handy guide to the sizing differences is given in the table below.

Dress Sizes

UK	8	10	12	14	16	18
US	6	8	10	12	14	16

Women's Shoes

UK	5	5.5	6	6.5	7
US	6	6.5	7	7.5	8

Men's Shoes

UK	7	7.5	8.5	9.5	10.5	11
US	8	8.5	9	10.5	11.5	12

Complaints
Make any complaints at a hotel, store or restaurant to the manager in a calm manner. For more serious complaints, contact the police, or report your problem to the tourist office *(see p 123)*.

Children playing in Battery Park.

Consulates *

Embassies and consulates can be found at the following addresses:

British Consulate
845 Third Ave.
☎ 212/745-0202

Australian Consulate
150 E. 42nd St.
☎ 212/351-6500

Canadian Consulate
1251 Avenue of the Americas,
☎ 212/596-1600

Irish Consulate
345 Park Ave.
☎ 212/319-2555

New Zealand Consulate
780 Third Ave.
☎ 212/832-7420

Crime

Crime in New York has decreased dramatically over the past ten years. As in many major cities, however, crimes do occur, and a few precautions should be taken:

- Try not to look too obviously like a tourist.
- Don't flash money around.
- Stick to busy tourist areas, especially at nighttime; find out which places or areas should be avoided.
- If confronted by a mugger, the best thing to do is to hand over whatever is being demanded; keep a small wad of money handy as a precaution – if you're confronted this might be sufficient to satisfy the mugger.
- Keep valuables locked in your hotel safe.
- Never open your hotel door to anyone if you don't know who it is.

If your passport is stolen, report it immediately to the nearest consulate. Keep travelers' checks separate from the list of their numbers, and in the event of theft, report their loss to the telephone number supplied.

Currency *see p 119*

Customs and Entry Regulations *see p 108*

Disabled Visitors

The US provides exceptional facilities for the disabled, thanks to the 1990 Americans with Disabilities Act. Most public transportation is equipped to take wheelchairs, and attendants accompanying disabled persons can often travel free. Disabled persons travel at half-fare on New York public transportation.

All public buildings must by

law be wheelchair accessible and provide suitable toilet facilities, and most street corners slope for easy access. Public telephones are easy to reach, and there are special stalls in public lavatories, Braille indicators in elevators, and an increasing number of reserved parking places.

Popular attractions generally cater to disabled visitors, and efforts are made to ease their path and provide necessary comforts. Tourist offices provide relevant information for disabled visitors *(see p 123)*, and local telephone directories list disabled support groups.

Larger hotels have specially designed hotel rooms which should be requested in advance. The major car rental companies provide cars with hand controls at no extra cost, although these are limited and advance reservation is advised.

All New York City Transit buses and some subway stations are wheelchair accessible. For information contact MTA Customer Assistance, 370 Jay Street, Room 720, Brooklyn, NY 11201 ☎ 718/596-8585. NYC Transit also operates a shared ride, door-to-door service for people with disabilities who are unable to use public transport. For

information about eligibility ☎ 877/337-2017.

A free guide to the city's cultural institutions, *Access for All* ($5), is obtainable from Hospital Audiences, Inc., 548 Broadway, 3rd Floor, New York, NY 10012; ☎ 212/575-7663 or 800/424-4685.

Driving *
Driving in the US is on the right-hand side. Foreign nationals may drive in the US on their own driving license, and fuel is cheap, compared to overseas. Speed limits are as follows: 15mph in school zones, 25mph in business and residential areas, and 55-70mph on the expressways (always follow posted limits). Remember that everyone in the car must wear a seat belt.

The majority of streets in Manhattan are one-way. Rush hours are 7am-9am and 4:30pm-6pm; roads will be most congested during these times.

Parking is very difficult in Manhattan, especially street parking on weekdays, and garage fees are high. Illegally parked vehicles are quickly towed away or ticketed. Look for a parking lot (car park) or designated meter parking, or leave your car in the hotel garage. In the event that your

Driving on New York's busy streets can be a daunting experience.

car is towed, the Parking Violation Bureau's Manhattan **Tow Pound** is located at Pier 76, W. 38th streets at 12th Avenue (☎ 212/971-0771).

For parking violations, call the city's Dept. of Transportation ☎ 212/225-5368. *See also pp 110 and 112.*

Electric Current *

All personal appliances run on 110 volts AC, and most sockets are designed to take flat two-pronged plugs. UK visitors will need an adaptor for their appliances, which may be bought from electrical goods stores or borrowed from the front desk of large hotels. Appliances rated for other voltages will need a transformer.

Embassies *see p 114*

Emergencies

Simply dial ☎ **911** in an emergency, and the appropriate emergency service will be summoned quickly. Try to give accurate directions, including hotel name, street name and nearest intersection if you can. Special telephone boxes have been installed on interstate highways at a quarter to a half-mile apart, and from one of these you can call for help without dialing 911. In cases of dire distress the Consulate might help.

Excursions

One of the best ways of seeing New York is on foot. The city's grid-like plan makes it easy to systematically scour any area you are interested in. To get an overview of the city, however, an organized tour lasting half a day or a full day is ideal.

Tour operators offer a wide choice of excursions *(see p 28)*, including sightseeing tours, guided walking tours, double-decker bus tours, helicopter rides, guided museum tours, and three-hour cruises around the island of Manhattan.

Details of these and other tours can be obtained from the publication *Official NYC Guide*, available free from the Times Square Visitors Center, Broadway between 46th and 47th streets *(open daily 8am-8pm)*.

Health *
Travel insurance is essential for foreign visitors to the US because there is no national health system to provide for medical needs, and private health care is extremely expensive. Travel agents and tour companies will recommend a suitable policy that should include at least $1,000,000 for medical expenses.

Should you have a serious accident during your stay, you will be cared for first and asked to pay later. To find a doctor,

Sightseeing along Broadway.

call **Physicians Home Care**
☎ 718/238-2100 or
Hotel Docs ☎ 800/468-3537.
Remember to keep all receipts
and documentation so that you
can claim back any sums you
pay out.

Walk-in medical and dental
clinics are listed in the
telephone directories, and for
minor problems drugstores
have a huge selection of
palliatives to offer. An
emergency dental service is
available (☎ 212/573-9502).

If you know in advance that
you will be needing medication
in the US, get your doctor to
make out a prescription for the
composition of your medicine,
not the brand name.

Information *see p 123*

Language *

English is the main language,
although most other languages
of the world are also spoken.
British visitors may find that
there is confusion about what
is meant by some British terms,
which can have a very different
meaning in the US
(*see chart below*).

American English	British English
restroom	*public toilet*
bathroom	*private toilet*
chips	*crisps*
broiled	*grilled*
sidewalk	*pavement*
trailer	*caravan*
do not pass	*no overtaking*
no standing	*no parking or stopping*
pants	*trousers*
to go	*take-away (food)*
shoulder	*lay-by*
purse	*handbag*
line	*queue*
subway	*underground*
drugstore	*chemist*
check	*bill*

Laundry

There are plenty of coin-operated laundromats and dry-cleaning establishments. Hotels also usually offer these services, albeit at a higher price.

Lost Property

Report any lost items as soon as you realize they are missing. In hotels, check with the front desk or hotel security; local telephone directories list the numbers of cab companies and public transportation. The police should be informed of any lost travel documents. Try to obtain a police report if you intend to file a claim for valuable items. Lost or stolen travelers' checks and credit cards should be reported immediately to the issuing company with a list of numbers, and the police should also be informed.

To claim property left in taxi cabs, contact the Taxi Commission (☎ 212/692-8294); you need the taxi receipt in order to trace the lost property.

Maps

The *Michelin Green Guide New York City* provides an overview map of New York, along with extensive information about the city. Free maps and brochures, as well as bus and subway maps, are provided by the main tourist centers *(see p 123)* and chambers of commerce. Car rental companies also provide free maps that will help with general route planning and driving.

The Michelin motoring map **No 491** USA North Eastern, scale 1/2,400,000 (1in=38mi), covers the northeast US. If you do go beyond the city limits, note that state and national parks issue maps of scenic drives, hikes and trails when you enter the park.

Medical Care *see p 117*

Money *

US currency is based on the decimal system, with 100 cents to the dollar. Dollar bills are all the same size and color – green – so check the different denominations carefully: they come in $1, $2, $5, $10, $20, $50 and $100. Coins are a dollar (100 cents), half-dollar (50 cents), a quarter (25 cents), a dime (10 cents), a nickel (5 cents) and a penny (1 cent).

The safest way to carry large amounts of money is in dollar travelers' checks, which are widely accepted and exchanged, or by using a credit card. Local taxes (NYC sales tax is 8.25%) are added on almost everything you buy – including meals – but are not necessarily part of the marked price, and there is also a city tax on hotel occupancy of 15.25% plus $2 per night, which is not included in the quoted rate. It is useful to carry single dollar bills for tips. *(see p 123).*

Newspapers

The city's own newspapers include *The New York Times*, *New York Daily News* and the *New York Post*, but newspapers from around the US and overseas are also available.

Weekly publications, *New York Magazine*, *The New Yorker*, *Time Out New York* and *The Village Voice*, include listings of events in and around town. Free copies of *City Guide* and *Where New York* are available from hotels and restaurants.

Opening Hours

Drugstores: 9am-7pm daily, with some open 24 hours. These include Duane Reade Pharmacy, 224 W. 57th Street at Broadway (☎ 212/541-9708) and RiteAid, 303 W. 50th Street (☎ 212/247-8384).
Stores: 10am-6pm, Mon-Fri; 10am-1pm or 6pm, Sat. Many large department stores open until late one or two evenings a week and some also open on Sunday.
Supermarkets: 8am-9pm or 10pm, Mon-Sat; 8am-7pm Sun.

Some are open 24 hours.
See also Post Offices and Banks.

Photography

Good-quality film and camera equipment are available throughout New York, and there are plenty of facilities for fast processing. Try to buy film from discount stores where possible, but check that expiration dates are still current.

Police *

American police are generally helpful and obliging when things go wrong. In an emergency ☎ 911. For non-emergency ☎ 646/610-5000 (Mon-Fri 9am-6pm). There are three types of police in the US: the City Police, the Sheriff whose domain is outside the city limits, and the State Police, who deal with traffic accidents and traffic violations beyond the city limits.

Post Offices

Local post offices are generally open from 9am-5:30pm, though these times may vary. Stamps may also be bought from machines at the post office or in business districts, or from hotels and drugstores. Mail boxes, painted blue, can be found on street corners.

Ordinary mail within the US

Brooklyn Bridge links the Financial District with Brooklyn.

costs 37 cents for a letter weighing up to one ounce. Air mail between the US and Europe takes about a week; postcards to Europe and aerogrammes cost 70 cents; letters weighing up to half an ounce are 80 cents.

The Main Post Office at West 33rd Street and Eighth Avenue is open 24 hours (☎ 212/330-3002). The Grand Central Railroad Terminal post office, 450 Lexington Avenue at 44th Street, is open 7:30am-9pm Mon-Fri, and 7:30am-1pm Sat.

Public Holidays

New Year's Day: January 1
Martin Luther King Jr's Birthday: 3rd Monday in January
Presidents' Day: 3rd Monday in February
Memorial Day: Last Monday in May
Independence Day: July 4
Labor Day: 1st Monday in September
Columbus Day: 2nd Monday in October
Veterans' Day: November 11
Thanksgiving Day: 4th Thursday in November
Christmas Day: December 25

On these days, shops, banks and offices are likely to be closed all day; in some places Good Friday is a half-day holiday.

Religion

New York is a melting pot of all the nationalities of the world, and just about every religious group is represented here. Catholic churches are easy to find, and most communities are served by churches of several denominations. There is also a flourishing Jewish community in New York.

For information on the different services available, check the listings in the Saturday *New York Times* or the *Yellow Pages* under "churches" or "synagogues."

Smoking

Smoking is frowned upon in the US. All public transport and public places are no-smoking zones, though some restaurants do include smoking sections.

Telephones *

The easiest way to make an overseas call is from a hotel room, and although this is more expensive than using a public telephone, it can save a lot of time and energy. You can also call collect or use your overseas credit card by dialing **0** for the operator. To dial direct from a public telephone, dial **011** plus the country code plus area code plus the telephone number. Make sure that you have a good supply of money in small coins or buy a prepaid calling card from a newstand or corner grocery. This is the cheapest option by far. The lowest rates for international calls to Europe are in effect between 6pm and 7am, and the same is true for long-distance calls within the US.

There are around 100 area codes in the US. To call outside your area code, dial **1** plus the area code plus the number. The rate for local calls will be posted in the telephone booth.

Time Difference

New York is in the Eastern Standard Time (EST) zone, which is five hours behind Greenwich Mean Time (GMT). Daylight Saving Time lasts from the first Sunday in April, when clocks are advanced one hour, until the last Sunday in October, when clocks are set back one hour.

Tipping *

Tipping is standard practice in the US. The accepted – and expected – rates are 15-20% in restaurants, 10-15% for taxis, 10-20% for hairdressers and barbers and 10-15% for bartenders and cocktail servers. Chambermaids should receive $2 for each day of your stay, porters about $1 per bag, and doormen $1 for hailing a cab. (A New Yorker's shortcut to working out a restaurant tip is to double the city sales tax shown on the bill, giving a tip of 16.5%.)

Toilets

Public toilets, such as those in parks, are probably best avoided, both from a cleanliness and a safety point of view. On the other hand, every public building must provide public toilets – known as rest rooms, powder rooms, or men's or women's room – and these are usually well maintained. Large stores, restaurants, hotels and most coffeeshops also have good facilities. In restaurants and theaters, where there is an attendant, a small tip will be expected.

Tourist Information Offices

There are two excellent sources of information that you can freely tap into when planning a visit to New York: the **United States Travel and Tourism Administration**, which has offices in US embassies and consulates throughout the

A more relaxing way of getting around in Central Park is by horse-drawn carriage.

world, and the **NYC and Company's Official Visitor Information Center**, 810 Seventh Avenue, New York, 10019 (☎ 212/484-1222 or ☎ 800/692-8474). Both offer a wide range of maps, brochures, guides and plans, plus information on accommodations, seasonal events, eating facilities, places of interest and sightseeing tours.

NYC and Company publishes the *Official NYC Guide* four times a year. It contains information on sights, accommodations, restaurants and many seasonal events. A copy can be requested from the bureau by mail in advance of your visit. To obtain a copy (free) in New York, stop by the Visitor Information Center, at 810 Seventh Avenue, or the **Times Square Visitors Center**, 46th and Broadway. This office, which has information on every aspect of touring in New York, is open daily, year-round, 8am-8pm.

Transportation

The best way to get around Manhattan is by foot, but the fastest way to get anywhere is to go by subway. The most interesting way of traveling – if sometimes the slowest – is on the city's buses.

Most people do their sightseeing via a mixture of all three, and the New York public transportation system is reasonably efficient. The fast pace of the city becomes positively frenzied during rush hours, however, and visitors are advised to avoid subways and buses from 7am-9am and 4:30pm-7pm.

The **subway** operates 24 hours a day, but several routes are available only at limited times. Routes and directions are shown on wall maps inside the station. Station entrances with a green globe at the street entrance are staffed around the clock; a red globe indicates restricted operating hours.

Most Manhattan routes are either Uptown (north) or Downtown (south) rather than across town, and electronic signs on the sides of trains show the starting and finishing points of the journey, as well as the line and route.

Local trains stop at every station, while express trains stop only at major stations. The cost of a one-way ride, regardless of length, is $1.50. Discount passes are also available. It may be worthwhile to buy a one-day Fun Pass ($4) or an unlimited-use 7-day MetroCard ($17). Tokens or MetroCards can be purchased inside the entrance to every station. Note that either can also be used on the buses.

Traveling by night is safest in the crowded central car on which you will usually find the conductor. Daytime trips on the subway are as trouble-free as on public transportation in any other major city.

Buses also cost $1.50 per trip, paid with exact change, a subway token or a MetroCard. Transfers between routes are free, but remember to ask the driver for a "transfer" if you pay with cash or a token.

Buses stop every two or three blocks, along most avenues and several of the larger cross-town streets, usually near the street corner. Route numbers are indicated at bus stops. Buses also have electronic signs displaying their number, route and destination.

Taxis, New York's famous yellow cabs, are in evidence everywhere, and they are reasonably priced. They can either be hailed in the street, or found outside hotels, theaters, stations and terminals.

Ferries take passengers to Staten Island and New Jersey, while Roosevelt Island is accessible by aerial tram from 60th Street and Second Avenue.

Vaccinations *see p 108*

Wall Street subway station.

Water

New York drinking water is
excellent. Most coffeeshops
and restaurants will serve a
glass of ordinary water as a
courtesy. If you prefer, there is
a wide variety of bottled water
available.

INDEX

Accommodations 83-86
Alice Austen House 70
Amato Opera Theater 98
American Ballet Theater 97
American Indians 12, 13, 14, 15
Andersen, Hans Christian (statue) 64
Aqueduct racetrack 107
Astroland 72
Atlantic Avenue 67
Attractions 37

Bagel shops 91
Bargemusic 98
Baseball 106
Basketball 107
Battery Park 36, 58
Battery Park City 58
Belmont Park racetrack 107
Belvedere Castle 63
Big Apple Greeter 28
Bloomingdale's 94, 95
Bowne House 70
Brighton Beach 74
Broadway 24, 100-101
Broadway Theater Guide 97
Bronx 10, 66
Bronx Zoo 60
Brooklyn 10, 67
Brooklyn Academy of Music (BAM) 68, 98
Brooklyn Botanic Garden 61
Brooklyn Heights Historic District 68
Brooklyn Historical Society 68

Calendar of Events 81
Carnegie Hall 46, 98
Castle Clinton 36, 60
Central Park 26, 62
Central Park Zoo 63
Chinatown 22, 32-33
Chrysler Building 46, 47
Churches 44-46
  Cathedral of St. John the Divine 46
  Church of the Ascension 32
  Plymouth Church of the Pilgrims 69

Saint Patrick's Cathedral 45
St. Paul's Chapel 46
Trinity Church 34, 35, 46
Circle Line tours 29
City Center Theater 98
City Hall 46
City Island 66
Cloisters 42
Coffeehouses 93
Coney Island 72
Coney Island Beach 74, 75
Conference House 71
Continental Airlines Arena 107
Corona Park 64
Cotton Club, The 102

Delicatessens 93
Discovery Garden 62

Electronics Boutique 95
Ellis Island 20, 26, 39
Empire State Building 26, 48, 49
Enchanted Forest, The 72
Entertainment and Nightlife 97-106

FAO Schwarz 72
Federal Hall National Memorial 16
Fifth Avenue 94
Financial District 34
Fire Island 75
Flatiron Building 18
Flushing Meadows-Corona Park 64, 106, 107
Food and Drink 87-93
Football 106

Garment District 96
Giants Stadium 106, 107
Gold Coast mansions 79
Grace Rainey Rogers Auditorium 98
Gracie Mansion 48
Grand Central Terminal 48, 50
Gray Line tours 29
Greenwich Village 31, 93

Hamptons 77
Historic Richmond Town 71
History 12-22
Horseracing 107
Hudson River Valley 79
Hyde Park 79

Ice hockey 107
Island Helicopter Sightseeing 28

Jacques Marchais Center of Tibetan Art 71
Jamaica Bay Wildlife Refuge 70
Jamaica Centre for Arts and Learning 70
Jazz 103, 106
Jones Beach State Park 75

Kingsland Homestead 70

Lefferts Homestead 69
Lincoln Center for the Performing Arts 50, 51
Long Beach 75
Long Island 74-79
Lyndhurst 79

Macy's 92, 95
Madison Avenue 94
Madison Square Garden 51, 106
Manhattan 9, 31-36
Manhattan Walks 31-36
Metropolitan Opera House 50, 98

Museums 37-44
  American Craft Museum 37
  American Museum of Natural History 26, 37
  American Museum of the Moving Image 37
  Brooklyn Museum of Art 38
  Children's Museum of Manhattan 39
  Cradle of Aviation 78
  Ellis Island Immigration Museum 20, 26, 39
  Fraunces Tavern Museum 34, 48
  Frick Collection 40
  Intrepid Sea-Air-Space Museum 50
  Isamu Noguchi Garden Museum 44
  Jewish Museum 40
  Metropolitan Museum of Art 26, 41-42
  Museum of Modern Art 26, 43

INDEX

National Museum of the American Indian 34, 36
New York Historical Society 43-44
New York Transit Museum 44
Museum of Television and Radio 43
Museum of the City of New York 43
Queens Museum of Art 44
Solomon R. Guggenheim 40
South Street Seaport Museum 54
Van Cortlandt House Museum 64
Vanderbilt Museum 78
Whaling museums 78
Whitney Museum of American Art 44

Nassau Memorial Coliseum 107
National Broadcasting Company (NCB) 30
New York Aquarium 72
New York Botanical Garden 60, 61
New York City Ballet 98
New York City Hall of Science 98
New York Public Library 25
New York Stock Exchange 34, 52
New York University 32

Oak Room 102
Off Broadway 100
Off-Off Broadway 100
Old Bethpage Restoration Village 78, 79
Orchard Street 94
Orient Point State Park 77

Pelham Bay Park 64
People and Culture 22
Philipsburg Manor 79
Plaza Hotel 111
Poe Cottage 66
Prospect Park 64
Provincetown Playhouse 32

Queens 10, 69
Radio City Music Hall 30
Robert Moses State Park 75
Rockaway Beach 74
Rockefeller Center 26, 52, 53, 84, 85
Rockefeller Plaza 53

Roosevelt Island Tramway 72

Sagamore Hill National Historical Site 78
Shea Stadium 106
Shopping 94-96
Snug Harbor Cultural Center 71
SoHo 96
Soldiers' and Sailors' Memorial Arch 64
South Street Seaport Historic District 54, 55
Spirit Cruises 29
Sports 106-107
Staten Island 11, 70
Staten Island Ferry 54
Statue of Liberty 19, 27, 54, 56
Stony Brook 78
Strawberry Fields 63

Tarrytown 79
Tennis 107
Theater District 100
Theodore Roosevelt Birthplace National Historic Site 52, 54
Times Square 100, 103
Times Square Visitors Center 124
Tours 28-30
  boat 29
  helicopter 28
  special interest 30
  walking 30-36
Trump Tower 94
UNICEF 96
United Nations Headquarters 55
US Open 107
USTA National Tennis Center 64, 107

Valentine-Varian House 66
Van Cortlandt Park 64, 66
Vietnam Veterans Memorial 56

Wall Street 34
Walt Whitman Birthplace State Historic Site 78
Washington Arch 32
Washington, George 16, 17
Washington Square 32
Wave Hill 66
Weather 80
West Point 79

Whale-watching cruises 78
William T. Davies Wildlife Refuge 71
Winter Garden 58
Woodlawn Cemetery 66
Woolworth Building 56-57
World Financial Center 58
World Trade Center Site 27, 58

Yankee Stadium 66, 106
Yonkers Raceway 107